REFUGE

Liane I. Brown

UP UNUSUAL PUBLICATIONS
® Greenville, South Carolina 29614

Refuge
by Liane I. Brown
© 1987 Unusual Publications

Printed in the United States of America.
95 94 93 92 91 90 89 88 87   5 4 3 2 1

ISBN: 0-89084-392-9

Library of Congress Cataloging-in-Publication Data

Brown, Liane I., 1934-
    Refuge.

        1. Brown, Liane I., 1934-   . 2. World War,
1939-1945—Personal narratives, German. 3. East
Prussia (Poland and R.S.F.S.R)—Biography.
4. Germans—East Prussia (Poland and R.S.F.S.R.)—
Biography.   I. Title.
D811.5.B776 1987   940.53'161'0924 [B]   87-21578
ISBN 0-89084-392-9

Cover Illustration by James A. Brooks

To the Lord, Who never fails us;
To my Father and Mother,
whose steadfastness in their Christian walk
is a constant inspiration to me;
To Dieter, Marlies, and Udo,
who were too young to remember;
and to countless Germans,
whose stories have never been told.

Contents

Preface

I have been asked hundreds of times what I appreciate most about being a citizen of the United States. My answer to that question is always the same—freedom. I have lived under an oppressive regime. Consequently, I now have a great love for my country.

This book is a "thank you" to the Lord for leading us to America, the land in which my family has found true freedom. It is also a "thank you" to many of our American friends who encouraged us to write about some of our experiences. May we never take our freedom for granted, and may we do everything to preserve it.

This book is based on my mother's written personal accounts, extensive interviews with Kaetchen, who lives in West Germany, and my own experiences. Every incident is true, and the names are real.

Division of the Third Reich

■ The border of Germany prior to August 1939.

█ The territory that became West Germany (Federal Republic of Germany) after the war.

█ The territory that became East Germany (German Democratic Republic) after the war.

█ The territories that became parts of Poland and the U.S.S.R. when the Third Reich fell.

NORTH SEA

DENMARK

Copenhage

Hamburg

GERMANY

NETHERLANDS

BELGIUM

● Bochum

● Frankfurt

LUX.

FRANCE

Munich ●

● Zurich

"A thousand shall fall at thy side, and ten thousand at thy right hand; but it shall not come nigh thee. . . . Because thou hast made the Lord, which is my refuge, even the most High, thy habitation."
Psalm 91:7, 9

German words and expressions

Vati - Daddy
Mutti - Mommy
Opi - Grandpa
Omi - Grandma
Herr - Mr.
Frau - Mrs.
Onkel - Uncle
Tante - Aunt
kaputt - broken, smashed
komm - come
dummkopf - dumbbell, blockhead
suppe - soup
danke schoen - thank you
auf wiedersehen - good-bye
Schaefle - little sheep

Russian words and expressions

rabota - work
daway rabotay - get to work

1
The Beginning of the End

"**F**rau Guddat!" A familiar deep voice called into our dimly lit bomb shelter. "Are you down there?"

Mutti (Mommy) called back an answer, barely loud enough to be heard. I saw a tall silhouette moving down the spiral stone steps, coming slowly toward us.

"Pastor Walter—what are you doing here?" Mutti sounded more weary than surprised.

"I had to come and see if you and your children survived through the night. Praise the Lord! He has been gracious in protecting you again."

"Yes," Mutti replied, "the Lord has been good to us. We are all safe."

One of the pastor's hands dropped almost unconsciously onto my little brother's head. His voice was hesitant when he finally spoke. "Four children and their mother are no longer on earth today. Last night they joined the angels in heaven." A long pause followed before he gave us more information. "They were the newest members of our church. In place of their house I found a large bomb crater, that has also become their grave. When I saw their geese still alive, standing on the rim of the crater, honking, it was rather difficult for me to understand God's ways."

"The baby was only fourteen days old!" Mutti said sadly as she drew Udo, my youngest brother, closer to her. "Why must the innocent suffer? Four children! What did they do to start this war? Why do we as civilians have to spend night after night in a cold bomb shelter while a war is being fought above us and the enemy is successful in destroying our very existence?"

Raising his bushy eyebrows, Pastor Walter was about to speak, but Mutti hastened on. "Please—wait!" she whispered. "Our air raid guard is just entering the cellar. He is a Nazi, and everyone fears him. I don't want him to report you!"

"Thank you for the warning, but I have learned to be careful about what I say." A shadow of a smile touched the pastor's face. "Seeing spies in the congregation during every service has taught me not to jeopardize my life or that of anyone else. I have had to learn to bridle my tongue without becoming a compromiser. Let's just have a word of prayer before I leave to check on others of our congregation."

"Pray for me, too!" a stranger pleaded. "Please pray for me! Both of my children were killed last night. My husband was shot at the front line four weeks ago. I have nothing to live for now! Nothing! Why didn't the bombs take me, too?"

The stranger's weeping and sobbing rent my young heart. Carefully stepping over sleeping children, bundles, and suitcases, Pastor Walter slowly made his way to the lady. He took her hand and besought the Lord to comfort and strengthen her now and in the coming days. The lady wept bitterly as he talked quietly to her.

When the guard turned on the lights, we realized that our shelter was packed with people. Some of them sat motionless on their suitcases; others lay on the cold cement floor. Those who had stumbled into our shelter during the night with burning clothes and bleeding hands and faces were writhing in pain. No one had had time to find cover. The bombs had fallen before the sirens were sounded. I thought back to the endless night before. Even though my ears had seemed to explode every time a bomb burst, I felt something miraculous had happened when I realized that we were still alive.

"We will go to my uncle's farm in the country today, Schaefle (little sheep)," Mutti told me. "For weeks we have spent every night in this damp cellar. It is becoming too unhealthy and difficult for all of us. We used to have time to rush down here before the bombs fell, but during the past few nights the enemies have become more skilled in their surprise attacks. I have prayed again and again for guidance, and I believe that this is what the Lord wants us to do. We'll walk to Omi's (Grandmother's) house— I trust the Lord has kept her safe last night also—and see if one of her friends can take us by wagon to the country. Even if the Nazis had not confiscated our car, it seems we would not be able to drive through town this morning. All the reports are rather grim in regard to what our beautiful city looks like today."

Insterburg was smouldering as Mutti and we four children scrambled over bricks, broken glass, and scorched beams to my grandparents' house. Many homes were still burning as people stood in shock in the streets and watched the final flaming destruction of their businesses and belongings. A few firemen were aiming their water hoses at the tallest flames. But what could a fire department accomplish in a catastrophe of this magnitude? It seemed as if the whole town was an inferno. Devastation was everywhere! The huge Lutherkirche on the Markt-platz, however, showed no scars from the worst attack ever on Insterburg. The radio told us that both American and Russian planes had bombarded our city last night. Fortunately, we found Omi to be all right, if very frightened and worn out.

We made it safely to my uncle's farm and, for a short while, life was very peaceful for us even though we could still hear the explosions in our hometown. In the distance we saw the "Christmas tree" flares the enemy placed in the sky at night to light up targets. I knew it was impossible for me to hear the sirens of Insterburg, but my ears were constantly filled with that eerie sound, and my body still anticipated being jolted by the impact of the bombs.

The day we arrived back in Insterburg, Mutti's friend Kaetchen came for a brief visit. She had just wanted to know if we were still alive. "We just returned home after seven days in the country," Mutti told her. "We could no longer endure living in the bomb shelter. Is everything still all right with you and the boys at the parsonage?"

"Yes, praise be to the Lord! Our small village has not been hit. I just came to Insterburg today to get my travel permit and to check on you and the children. I plan to move to my father's house in Lippehne until it is safe to return to East Prussia. I am sure the enemy will never seize a town that close to Berlin. Our armed forces won't let that happen. But right here we are living too close to the Russian border and might be overrun any day should our front lines weaken."

"Do you really think that could happen? We are being told every day that an enemy will 'never set foot on East Prussian soil.' "

"I used to believe that, Emmy, but I no longer do. Things are becoming too critical at the border. Why don't you and your children come with me to Lippehne?"

"Kaetchen, do you really mean it? I have been asking the Lord for guidance for days now. I know we have to leave here, but I had no idea where we could go. We just can't take the nightly bombings anymore. All of my relatives live in the northern part of East Prussia, as you know. Some of them live in Berlin, but neither of those places is safe right now. Are you really serious about your offer, Kaetchen?"

"Of course."

"Thank you, *thank you*, Kaetchen! Your offer is an answer to prayer!" Mutti went to her friend and hugged her. "But will your dad have room for all of us? I am planning to take my mother-in-law with us wherever we go—I can't leave her here alone in this burning city."

"My dad's farm is small, and he has lived there alone since my mother's death. His house is not very big either, but his heart is. I am sure he'll take us all in. I'll write to him today and tell him that you are coming. In the meantime, God be with you till we meet again! We have a great God! He will protect all of us. And He will watch over our husbands, too, wherever they might be defending our country right now."

"See you in Lippehne!" Mutti called as Kaetchen walked out of the house.

Several days later on a cool night in August, Mutti, my grandmother, my two brothers, my sister, and I packed into a crowded train. Our papers had been checked during the daylight hours, and we had been told in which car to ride. Many crying mothers and children were turned away because they did not have travel permits. Hoping to jump a train and escape to the West, some of them had been camping at the railroad station for days.

4

At midnight the train finally began to move slowly out of the station. It was an unusual night for our town. There were no "Christmas trees" in the sky above. No bombs were whizzing through the air. No sirens were causing our hearts to jump from fear as the train engine pulled us along in utter darkness.

Beautiful Insterburg! It was Vati's (Daddy's) hometown, the city where all the Prussian kaisers were crowned. Trakehner horses had made it world-famous. The many lovely parks and man-made lakes gave recreation to its fifty thousand inhabitants. My brothers, my sister, and I were born there, but as our train crawled out of the city that night, everything was in turmoil. Thousands had lost their lives during the past few weeks. In the darkness of the night one could still see yellow flames, briefly shooting into the air to light up chaotic ruins before vanishing again.

It was raining in torrents the next afternoon as our train, bulging with homeless and hungry people, pulled into Lippehne. War had not yet reached this town near Berlin. It seemed strange to see all the buildings intact. The rain and damp air were refreshing after the stuffy train ride, and our hearts became peaceful. But how would we ever make any progress if the wheels of the baby carriage continued to fall off and roll into the gutter? This wartime carriage appeared to be made of cardboard. With everyone's help, however, our drenched group of refugees arrived at the old pastor's house.

"Shall I knock on the door?" Mutti asked us with hesitation in her voice. Her natural curls were even curlier now that they were wet. "I don't know the man! What will we do if he does not take us in? Where will we go? We are homeless! You children don't have a father, I don't have a husband, and we have no home!" She paused for a moment and took a deep breath. "But we have a God in heaven who watches over us."

With her right hand Mutti wiped some of the rain off her face, then knocked on the green door. Omi stood next to me with her head bowed. She must have been praying. After the longest moments in our lives, the farm door opened. The elderly gentleman inside looked bewildered by our drenched group and my crying little brother.

"Guten Tag, Herr Lehmann! I am Emmy Guddat, a friend of your daughter, Kaetchen. We are the ones Kaetchen wrote you about—she told you we would be coming."

5

The kind-looking man scrambled for words. "I have not heard from my daughter in several weeks. Her letter must have been lost. But come on in! Get out of the rain!"

After brushing some of the water out of our soaked clothes, we entered the long hallway. Mutti told Mr. Lehmann why we had left Insterburg and asked if it would be possible for us to stay with him until our hometown became safe again.

"Of course! You are welcome in my home—you may stay here as long as you like! And please call me Onkel (Uncle) Lehmann," the elderly preacher told us with a smile and twinkling eyes.

Mutti was visibly touched by the stranger's selfless response. With tears welling up in her eyes and a choking voice she said, "Thank you! Thank you, Onkel Lehmann! I don't know what else I can say."

Mutti then shared with Kaetchen's father that she and his daughter had met in the hospital in Insterburg when their oldest sons were born. She told him about the bombing attacks and that Kaetchen and his two grandsons were still living safely in their parsonage in the country. They were presently awaiting permission from the government to move to Lippehne. His son-in-law, the preacher, was still somewhere serving his country, and Kaetchen had not heard from him in some time. When she finished, Onkel Lehman showed us the part of the house where we would stay.

"I will let you make yourselves at home in the two rooms on the second floor," he said as he motioned for us to follow him upstairs. "Here we are. These are your rooms. They are rather small, but I think you will be able to manage."

"We will, and thank you so very much!"

"Mutti, look! Beds! Real beds!" Dieter burst out. "Can I go to bed now? No more bunks in the air raid shelter! Look, Mutti! Look!"

"Yes, you may take a nap, Dieter. But first you must take off your wet clothes! Open your rucksack and take out dry clothes—at least I hope they are still dry."

"I will! I will, Mutti!"

In his excitement he could hardly open the buckle of his rucksack and didn't seem to mind at all when Omi came to his rescue.

"Does Onkel Lehmann have animals on his farm, Mutti?"

"I don't know, son. You can ask him later."

This home was so peaceful! Thank you, Lord! No sirens pierced our ears. We didn't hear airplanes above us. There seemed to be nothing to fear. Our rooms in our Insterburg home had been huge, but right then I was glad to trade them and the shelter for these tiny ones.

Just as we finished changing into dry clothes, the preacher invited us downstairs for cake, coffee, and goat's milk. Some of his church friends had dropped in, and we learned that it was Onkel Lehmann's birthday. He received gifts of flowers, homemade cakes, and all types of food.

We hadn't seen real joy in anyone with whom we had been in contact recently, and I felt totally overwhelmed by seeing these people bubbling over with the joy of the Lord. They sang hymns and talked for hours about the blessings of the Lord.

My soul was in turmoil, though. How could it be so peaceful here when my hometown in East Prussia was lying in almost total ruin? Insterburg was a German city, just like Lippehne. It didn't make sense to me. Was Hitler really the cause of all these problems as some adults said? I wondered why our leader wasn't protecting our country and us. In the Hitler Youth, I learned that our Fuehrer loved us, and we should return his love with all our hearts. Only by following him would we bring true happiness and fulfillment to our lives. How I had enjoyed all the marching and the sports programs! Being fit to follow our leader was every young person's goal.

But why was I so confused? Why did I have to leave my home and my friends? Onkel Lehmann was a very kind man, and I liked his little farm, but I'd rather be home and have things the way they used to be.

"Liane," Mutti asked, "what are you dreaming about? Would you like another piece of Onkel Lehmann's birthday cake?"

"Yes, please, Mutti."

Within a few days, we began to grow acquainted with Lippehne. It was a picture-postcard town, almost completely surrounded by three big lakes. Private gardens and promenades hugged the shore lines. Onkel Lehmann had gardens located at two of the lakes, one of which had a small cottage nestled under big apple trees near the water. A short boardwalk led

7

through the reeds to his tied-up boat and the open water. Dieter loved to catch crabs with his hands in the shallow, sandy lake bottom.

Since Mutti had never prepared crabs, Onkel Lehmann taught her how to cook the delicacy. During the week, Mutti and Omi helped the preacher with the garden work and the canning while Dieter and I attended school. After church on Sundays, when the weather was favorable, we all rowed the boat around the lakes. Our new friends joined us with their boats, and in parade-like fashion we paddled from one lake to another, singing hymns and folk songs and enjoying God's creation. It was great for us children to dangle our feet over the side of the boat and have them pulled through the cool water.

Onkel Lehmann was a wonderful teacher, and Dieter quickly learned how to feed and milk the goats. The two friends had such good times when working in the barn. I often sat on the hay and watched them. Does Onkel Lehmann miss his wife as much as Mutti misses Vati? I wondered.

"Tante (Aunt) Lehmann went to heaven two years ago," he told me when I asked him. "I miss her very much. But now the Lord has sent you to help me here, and I am so thankful for that. I don't know how I ever managed before all of you came."

One bright morning, Mutti told us that it was Udo's birthday. "Happy birthday, my little son!" Mutti said to her youngest child. "You are getting to be a big boy. You are one year old today. Let's see if you can take your first steps all by yourself. Oops! Down he goes!" Mutti helped Udo stand up and he tried again, but he couldn't take more than two steps at a time.

In the afternoon we all celebrated Udo's birthday at a park along the lake. It was a warm day, and instead of sitting on the blanket that was spread out on the lawn, we children preferred to sit on the grass. Udo looked so cute on his special day in short brown pants and an orange pullover. His hair was blond and straight like mine, and he was always happy and playful.

"Omi, your carrot cake is so-o-o good! May I have another piece?" Dieter begged.

"Of course, you may." As she cut a piece for him, my hand reached for another one also.

"I wonder where Emil is on this twenty-fifth day of August," Mutti said to her mother-in-law. "I wish he could see his son today, and his other three children too. Four months is a long time for children not to see their father."

"Yes, Emmy, I was just thinking about him. I can't stop praying for him and his safety. The Lord has been so good to all of us and has protected us from the bombs in Insterburg. I know He will reunite all of you. I just pray that it will be soon. You and Emil have been faithful and true to the Lord, and our God has promised to honor and bless those who really love Him and live for Him. I know that He will do that."

"Mutti, look! Quick, quick, look! Udo is walking!" Dieter called excitedly. "He is walking all by himself!" Indeed he was. We all sat and watched. My little brother looked so proud as he waddled through the grass without assistance.

At times Mutti looked rather discouraged, and she seldom smiled. She continued to write to Vati but never received a letter from him. Hearing bombs explode in the distance caused her and all of us to become more solemn again. The earth would shake and our windows would rattle. We began to wonder if bombs would hit Lippehne, too. "We must pray much for Vati," Mutti told us.

The months passed slowly. Then, on a cold, windy day in November, Kaetchen and her two sons arrived in our new hometown. Onkel Lehmann was thrilled to welcome his daughter and grandsons. For hours we celebrated their homecoming, even though they were very tired from the long train ride. Mutti became more cheerful again now that she could talk to her friend.

"Schaefle," Mutti said one day, "Kaetchen has offered to help take care of you children while I make a quick trip back to Insterburg. I want to see if I can bring some of our belongings to Lippehne. I especially need my sewing machine. It will be a little extra work for you, but I know you will be able to manage for a few days. What do you think?"

"That will be fine with me as long as you promise to come back. If a bomb hits your train or you are captured by the Russians, what are we going to do then?"

"Trust in the Lord, my daughter! Trust in the Lord! He will take care of you and me and Vati. Do you believe that?"

"I'll try, but it is hard not to worry about you."

After Mutti returned from Insterburg, she was not the same Mutti who had left. She seemed different somehow. Her face looked

9

sad and tired. "One side of our house has been ripped away by bombs, but I was still able to get my sewing machine and a few other things. Those possessions don't mean anything though, Kaetchen. It is all earthly stuff. What does it matter whether we have it or not?"

"What happened, Emmy? Why are you so depressed?"

"I can't get out of my mind what I heard about the small village of Nemmersdorf in East Prussia."

"Nemmersdorf! That is not far from Insterburg. What happened there?"

"Well, the atrocities that occurred in that village are beyond description. Everybody in Insterburg is talking about it, and I haven't been able to sleep well since I heard those reports."

"Perhaps, Emmy, we shouldn't talk about something that troubles you so."

"Oh no, Kaetchen, I believe we have to talk about it. We have to pray that these things will not happen to us."

"All right. I leave it up to you then."

"Well, when the Russian front broke into Germany for the first time along the border of East Prussia, the troops stormed into the village and started massacring civilians. All the women and young girls, down to the age of eight, were first raped and then either shot or dismembered. Several were raped and nailed to barn doors, naked. When the Germans regained control of that part of East Prussia, forty-eight hours later, they did not find one civilian alive. All the men, women, and children had been murdered. Two of the villagers were found later in another town. They were the only ones who managed to escape."

"That is just horrible, Emmy. Now I see why you are so worried. This can happen to anybody who is still in East Prussia." Kaetchen's face was grave. "Aren't you glad we came to Lippehne? But think of our friends and your relatives back there! How we must pray for them."

"Yes, we must. We must pray without ceasing."

"Tell me, though, Emmy. Couldn't these stories be just rumors?"

"Oh no, they aren't. A nurse who lives in Insterburg is from Nemmersdorf. When she heard about the massacre, she went to her village to check on her parents. She found her seventy-four-year-old father and seventy-two-year-old mother among the bodies of the villagers. There are many other witnesses, too."

"How can Hitler let this happen to his people? This is inconceivable!" Mutti and Kaetchen continued to talk, but I no longer heard what they said. My mind was on the gruesome war account. Would the Russians do that to us if they overran us? Everybody said they would never come as far as Lippehne. But what would happen if they did? Would we all be murdered? Why was there always so much talk about death when I had barely begun to live?

The refugees continued to flood into Lippehne, providing me with plenty of food for thought. My aunt, the wife of Vati's twin brother, came among them one day. Eventually, she and Omi moved into a house with some kind people directly across the street from Onkel Lehman's farmhouse—which was beginning to get very crowded. December brought us another friend from Insterburg: Emil Schmidtke, the choir director of our old church. He and his wife had both made plans, way back last summer, to meet in Lippehne if the war should separate them. He took up residence in the attic of Onkel Lehmann's house. My parents had been friends with "Onkel Emil" for a long time, so, with so many of our own people and old friends around, Lippehne was seeming even more like home. I still couldn't keep my thoughts off the terrible stories we'd heard, though. I spent much of my time thinking about it, and one day my preoccupied mind got me in trouble at school.

Dieter's and my school was located right across the street from us, and we could dash to class in seconds. My classmates, however, had built strong relationships with their friends throughout their lives and didn't want to associate with me. I had been assigned a seat in the very last row of the classroom. Our hands had to be placed on the desk, one on top of the other, at all times; only when we raised them to participate in answering or asking questions, or when we were writing, were we permitted to change their position. The teachers here were as strict as those in Insterburg, and they demanded total obedience. Each one of them had to be greeted with an outstretched, raised arm and the words "Heil, Hitler." It didn't matter where one met them— in town or somewhere on the school grounds. Upon the teacher's

11

entrance into the classroom, all the students jumped to their feet, stood at attention, and greeted him.

It was difficult for me to adjust to the new school, especially with so many new and troubling events to think about. My grades were satisfactory, I suppose, but I didn't have a sense of belonging. One day I found myself not raising my arm to say "Heil, Hitler" with the rest of the class. The teacher noticed that immediately and called me to the front. Forty students turned to stare at me as I made my way out of my seat toward him.

"You didn't say 'Heil, Hitler'!" he yelled, his face bright red with anger. "You disobeyed this teacher! You showed defiance for our country's leader! Why? Why? Why-y-y?" With his shouts echoing from the walls, he slapped my face so hard that I almost lost my balance. My head pounded and ached with pain, and the teacher's red finger marks still burned my face when I returned home from school that afternoon. The incident took place twelve days after my eleventh birthday.

Throughout the following day, thunder-like sounds could be heard in the distance while homeless people continued to pour through our town. They were not well liked, although some people were kind to them anyway. The original residents of Lippehne wished the refugees would just go back where they came from. The displaced, bewildered people met with much suspicion from many townspeople: why had they come? Couldn't they have stayed at home? Where would they live? Were they going to eat our food? Did they have money? Why did they all look so poor, dirty, and tattered? Few had any answers to these questions, but *we* knew why they had come! We continually heard of clashes between residents of Lippehne and the refugees, however. School was canceled and the unwelcome visitors moved into the school buildings and gym by the hundreds. That change of events pleased *me*. At least I didn't have to face that cruel teacher for a while.

2
Cross-Fire!

The rumblings of war seemed to be following the refugee treks toward our town. In the distance, exploding bombs once again caused the sky to light up at night as airplanes rumbled and whined through the sky. Roars from the approaching battles set all of Lippehne to trembling. "It feels like an earthquake," people said. "Is this going to be the beginning of the end?"

Broadcasting over the radio throughout the day, the mayor assured us, "We will alert our citizenry of danger and announce the safety measures the town has taken to protect the public should anything unforeseen happen."

"Schaefle, please take care of your brothers and sister for an hour or so. I want to go to city hall and see what kind of emergency preparations our town has made for us," Mutti told me.

"You have to bundle up, Mutti," I suggested. "It is bitter cold outside today."

We had barely settled down in the warm living room to play school when Mutti returned, frozen through and through and rather upset.

"What is the matter, Emmy?" Kaetchen asked. "What happened? What did they say to you?"

"Do you really want to know what Herr Schwarz, the Nazi official, said to me? While sitting smugly behind his polished desk, he glanced at me over his gold-rimmed glasses, leaned forward, and said without feeling, 'My dear Frau Guddat, as the brave wife of a German soldier, surely you are not going to panic! Those refugees from the East who have flooded our town should be chased back where they came from. They are here just to upset the people! Your fear of falling into the hands of the Russians is totally unnecessary.

'Everything is in readiness in case of danger. Special trains and buses are at the railroad station to transport mothers and children to safety. These precautions have been taken just in case the enemy should advance as far as Lippehne, but we don't foresee that at all. So don't worry! Just go home to your children and remain calm. There is absolutely no danger!' "

That conversation took place on January 29, 1945, at 12:00 P.M. By 2:00 P.M. the news was racing like brush fire through the streets that everyone must evacuate the city within two hours. "Let's try to be ready to leave in fifteen minutes, Kaetchen." Mutti was already flying about the house. "The train will be too crowded if we get there any later."

"Yes, I agree. We have to get there early."

After putting on several layers of winter clothing, I dressed my sister while Mutti bundled up Udo. We quickly grabbed our green rucksacks that had been packed for days and dashed downstairs. Onkel Lehmann said a brief prayer before we left.

Outside the house we put my seventeen-month-old brother and four-year-old sister in a wooden box that was placed on top of the sled. The railroad station was only two miles away. Mutti pulled the sled with one hand, struggling with two bundles in the other. Dieter and I helped steady the load as best we could, but again and again the sled tipped over in the ten inches of freshly fallen snow. The little ones were crying by the time we finally fought our way to the end of our street.

But why were these people coming toward us? I wondered. The railroad station was located in the direction we were going.

"No trains! No trains at the station!" sobbed one woman. She was almost bent to the ground, struggling to pull a handcart in which her old mother was seated. The older lady looked lifeless from the cold.

"They lied! They lied! The Nazis lied to us!" yelled someone else. "They all took off by train at one o'clock! Liars! Liars! We'll all die, and they are safe. "

As these reports registered in the shocked minds of people all around, many decided to return to their homes. Others like us, in disbelief, continued to battle the snow toward the railroad station. My little brother and sister were crying constantly. They continued to topple off the sled and their faces were red from the stinging snow.

"Mutti, I want to go home. I am cold," pleaded my oldest brother. The struggle was too much even for a seven-year-old. In the distance we heard bombs exploding and rumblings that sounded like thunder.

"Frau Guddat!" called a neighbor, who with her two children was stomping through the snow against the stream of people. "My children and I are just coming back from the station. There is not one train on the tracks. Thousands of people are at the station. They are freezing and crying and still waiting for a train. We have decided to go back home." She reached us and we all halted. "Hitler will come and hold the enemy back. I don't believe that our leader will forsake us. He will help us. You'll see. He'll come with his secret weapons and push the enemy back. In the meantime we'll be safe at home."

Kaetchen and her sons were also suffering from the cold. "Let's all return home," she suggested. "We can't get very far in this snow, and where will we spend the night if we do continue in this trek? It will be dark in a short time."

"I agree." Mutti's weariness could be heard in her voice. "Let's all go home, get a good night's rest, and start out early in the morning."

Silently, except for the little ones crying, our group began to struggle back to the small farm. We noticed that all of our neighbors were returning home also.

Moments before we reached the farm, shocking news began traveling from person to person: We must surrender! Only surrender will save us and our town! White flags have to be hung out of the windows!

"Surrender?" Onkel Emil shouted. "Where is Hitler with his army and secret weapons? Can't he defend our country?" Everyone was stunned by the news that we must surrender.

15

After shaking the snow off our clothes and shoes, we went into the living room, where I tried to calm my little sister and brother. Both had wet, icy faces, and their fingers and toes were red and puffy. In their suffering, they sobbed so hard that their little bodies trembled. While Onkel Lehmann rekindled the fire in the tile stove, Mutti and Kaetchen hurriedly ripped flags of surrender from white sheets.

"Surrender? What does that really mean?" Mutti asked everyone. "Are we just handing ourselves over to the enemy? That is the most terrible act possible for any human being. Are we handing ourselves over to the Russians? We can't do that! We have to get away from here! Will Lippehne become another Nemmersdorf? The thought is simply unbearable!"

"We tried to get away, Emmy, and you saw how far we got." Kaetchen's face was drawn and white.

I was lost in my own horrible thoughts while Mutti and Kaetchen silently hung the flags of surrender out of the windows on the two sides of the corner house that faced the streets. Suddenly a great explosion caused the whole house to shake. Fear brought everyone scrambling to the living room. As we all tried to get seated near the stove, someone knocked rapidly on the front door. Onkel Lehmann went to open it.

"May we stay with you tonight, Herr Lehmann? My children and I are afraid!" we heard an anxious voice pleading.

"Of course! Come on in!"

Everyone in the room extended a warm welcome to the neighbors. In our unlit room they appeared as shadows because, just as in Insterburg, there was blackout at night so that enemy bombers could not find our city. Not long after the neighbors' arrival, Omi and my aunt arrived to stay with us until we all knew for sure what was going to happen. We all settled down as best we could, no one saying a word, but just listening to the thundering explosions moving closer and closer to Lippehne.

Mutti and the four of us were huddled on the couch. At one point, I heard part of her whispered prayers: "Lord, please take all of us! Don't let one of my children stay behind alone!"

I hoped Mutti didn't mean what she was praying! As another bomb whistled through the air, I knew I should hide my tears, but hearing Mutti's prayer brought new fear to my heart. I didn't want to die. I was scared to die. How would I die? Would I be shot? Would a bomb fall on us? Suddenly I just couldn't feel my body anymore. Yes, I thought a bomb would be best.

More rapid knocking on the door caused everyone to become restless. More neighbors were seeking refuge at the old preacher's house. It didn't bother him that they had always mocked him. They had called him a religious fanatic, a religious nut, and a strange man, but in his heart he had forgiven them long ago and welcomed everyone in. Our living room was really becoming crowded now. There were twenty-nine people crowded into the small space.

"Please pray for me," requested an unfamiliar voice. "I don't know how to pray."

The earth was trembling, the house vibrating, and the windows rattling. The enemy was approaching our town.

"O Lord! Creator of us all!" prayed Onkel Lehmann. "You see us and know our fearful hearts. We're utterly helpless without You. We are in Your presence even now. We don't know what the next hours will bring, but please make this house an ark of safety for all of us. Fill us with Your peace!"

Sobbing could be heard in every corner of our room; yet Mutti was peaceful. I could sense her peace. My aunt was probably crying, too. Her husband, Vati's twin, had been killed just a short time ago while defending Insterburg. Now, we had only two men in the house: Onkel Lehmann and Onkel Emil, who was an invalid from World War I. He had an artificial leg.

Even though the rumbling increased with the lengthening of the night, the younger children were sleeping. We sat silently for hours and listened to the war advance. The Russians were nearing our town rapidly. Then our ears detected a new, unfamiliar sound.

"Those are cannons," Onkel Emil informed us. "They are beginning to shoot at Lippehne."

One huge explosion followed another. Suddenly light flooded the house through the bedroom window and spilled into the living room. A neighbor went to look out of the window.

"The sky is aglow!" she called. "All the buildings on the other side of the lake are on fire!"

I rushed out of my seat to take a quick look. The bright, yellow flames that appeared to touch the sky gave me the most horrible feeling. The frames of the homes resembled black

17

skeletons. My heart raced when I realized that no one could escape those sweeping sheets of fire. I tried to snuggle back on the couch next to Mutti, but my body trembled and my mind was in turmoil. How many people were perishing in those flames? I wished my mind would just fall asleep, but it was wide awake.

"O God! O God, save us!" someone prayed out loud.

"Yes, save us! Save us!" voices muttered throughout the room.

Some of those who had never trusted in the Lord before were trying to strike bargains with Him now. "If you get me out of this, God, I will become a better person. Help, God! Help! Don't kill us, God!"

"Why doesn't Hitler come with his secret weapons?" others wondered.

Still others showed their bitterness. "I thought You were supposed to be a loving God! Why then are You doing this to us?"

Another voice pleaded, "I don't know how to pray. Please pray for us, Herr Lehmann!"

The tracks of tanks were beginning to clank on the cobblestone pavement of Main Street. Since our home was only one block away, it vibrated continuously. Long had been the nights in the bomb shelter, and scary, but this night was eternity. It dragged on as my fear of the Russians increased. If only it were morning! Things would not be so frightening and hopeless then. Somehow, I knew, we would be rescued by our leader.

I must have fallen asleep from sheer exhaustion because suddenly loud noises awakened me. It sounded as if the house door was being broken down. All at once we heard hollering and yelling in the hallway. An angry mob of men kicked the door to the living room open, burst in, and aimed their flashlights at our eyes. I saw nothing but guns and bayonets pointing at us. Soldiers! Russian soldiers were in our house! Their eyes flew from person to person. No German soldiers here—only two old men.

"Watch! Watch! If not watch, everything kaputt!" The demand was clear. Everyone took off his watch and handed it to the enemy. Dropping them into their pants' pockets, they stormed out of the room, through the hallway, and out of the house. Onkel Emil told us that these were Mongolian soldiers because their skin was tan-colored and their eyes somewhat slanted.

There was a hush over the whole room. Our men closed the front door and jammed it with a heavy log, but almost immediately another group of soldiers kicked it open again, and ran shouting through the house in search of German men. "Watch! Watch!" they screamed when they found us all cowering in the living room. No one moved to give them a watch. That infuriated them. "Watch! Watch!" they hollered even louder. One of them then tried to explain to us what he was after by pushing up his sleeve and exposing about ten watches on his hairy lower and upper arm.

"We don't have watches. Your comrades already took our watches," Onkel Lehmann tried to tell them, but they did not understand. As they became even more enraged, Kaetchen slipped into the kitchen, which was right next to the living room, and in seconds returned with a plate of cookies. She offered them to the soldiers. That move really startled them. They made her eat some first before they devoured the rest. Then, surprisingly enough, they left the house.

For hours tanks rumbled through town and Russians searched our little farm. Occasionally shots rang out in the streets. After the first few hours under Russian occupation, the soldiers' demands changed. "Woman, come!" they began commanding. But none of our ladies ever moved. They all hid their faces. No one wanted to look beautiful. One of the neighbor ladies sat with folded hands and moving lips when a Russian aimed his flashlight at her face. She must have learned to pray. Shooting outside, however, suddenly distracted the troops. They turned on their heels and stumbled out of the house.

While our two men were busy securing the front door, the women tried to make themselves ugly. They dug ashes from the kitchen stove to smear on their faces, and they messed up their hair. Mutti dashed upstairs, put on black pants, and covered her head with a black scarf. Everybody was huddling back in the living room again when the next band of soldiers broke through the front door barricade and crashed into the hallway. Of course, all the children were awake by then, and the women were pretending to busy themselves with their little ones when the warriors stomped into the room.

"Woman, come!" one soldier yelled at Mutti, but she remained seated on the chair with Udo on her lap.

"Woman, come!" he commanded even louder.

She didn't move. Then the Russian placed his pistol at Onkel Emil's forehead. No one in the room seemed to be breathing. Even the little ones were silent. Suddenly my four-year-old sister pulled away from me and ran to the Russian. She stretched her little arms toward him and wanted him to pick her up. He was so shocked that he almost dropped his pistol. Furiously he pushed Marlies back. She fell down, and he stumbled out of the room.

"Thank you, Lord," Onkel Lehmann prayed out loud, "for sending Your angel to watch over us. Continue to keep us safe!"

In the dim light of dawn we made plans to protect ourselves. Onkel Lehmann showed the young girls a trap in the bedroom floor. "That door leads to a small room in the basement," he said. "The oval braided rug shall cover that door at all times. It will be Dieter and Liane's job to pull the rug over the escape the second you have slipped into the cellar. The front door will be locked and bolted and opened only by Onkel Emil. Since he can't walk very fast with his prosthesis, the ladies will have enough time to hide."

It was almost daylight by then, and the tanks were still rattling through town. The house vibrated continuously. We didn't hear any troops outside and used the time for a quick dress rehearsal. The teenage girls learned that it was rather difficult to slide into the basement speedily and not fall off the steep steps.

Right in the middle of our practice session, gun butts were slamming against the front door. Onkel Emil hobbled through the long hallway to see about the ruckus. While we heard all the abuse the Russians hurled at him for moving so slowly, Dieter and I quickly pulled the rug over the trap door. With lightning speed we zipped to the living room and helped care for the little ones. The troops, dressed in olive green uniforms and fur hats, raced from room to room and out into the barnyard in search of German men. Omi and Kaetchen were busy with the children, while most of the young mothers had hidden somewhere. Kaetchen was only five feet tall and pretended not to be very bright. She always smiled at the Russians and offered them something to eat. This tactic never failed to shock them.

The first day under Russian occupation seemed utterly hopeless and endless. Onkel Emil informed us that we were now dealing with White Russians. Their searching techniques were the same as the others though: running, shouting, kicking furniture and walls, hollering and screaming, and scaring us by pointing their rifles or pistols at us. They managed to be successful in frightening even the smallest child. All of the children cried almost continuously.

Throughout the next few days the stream of enemies flooding our house was endless. At one time the girls were in the basement for several hours. There was no heat in the cellar, and it was rather difficult for them to be in that musty room for so long, but considering the alternative, no one complained. The days and nights dragged by without rest for anyone. Fear of the soldiers' demands for women still gripped everyone's heart. Miraculously, however, the Lord had provided protection for each lady and girl.

One morning, finally, it looked as if we would have a few hours of peace. Most of our group were completely exhausted and asleep on the living room floor. The children were awake and had gathered in the kitchen for lunch. Onkel Lehmann was just beginning to give thanks for the meal when the front door was almost beaten down. Everyone scrambled toward his hiding place. Dieter and I ran to our assigned post. The girls were slower than usual in letting themselves into the cellar because they were still half asleep. My brother and I were still straightening out the rug when three soldiers rushed in. One of them pulled me off the floor by my arm, lifted up the rug, and opened the wooden lid. The girls were cowering in one corner as guns pointed at them and a flashlight shone into their eyes.

"You spy! You spy! You not kill us! We kill you!" one of the soldiers shouted, cocking his rifle and aiming it at the trembling girls.

"We are not spies!" the girls cried. "We are not spies!"

Kaetchen sensed danger and rushed into the bedroom. She tried to tell the soldiers that the girls were hiding because they were afraid. "Afraid! Afraid!" she repeated. But they didn't understand. Another soldier brought his rifle up, imitating his companion's actions.

"Lord, help them understand," Kaetchen whispered under her breath. As she spoke, the soldiers suddenly, as if on command, withdrew their rifles, turned, and left. White as sheets, sobbing, and almost fainting, the girls emerged from their dungeon. I sat where I had fallen, rubbing my arm and watching in amazement as I realized that we had again been spared the horrors that all others in the town were enduring.

3
New Troubles

Our house was still filled with people, and the food supply dwindled rapidly. It was decided that we would eat only two meals a day, the last one at 2:30 P.M. Church services were held in the living room at the onset of darkness, about 4:00 P.M. Since the whole town was without electric power now, Onkel Lehmann read from the Bible by candlelight. After his reading, one of the children blew out the candle. This small task was always the highlight of the service for the little ones. As for myself, I loved hearing the adults tell of God's leading in their lives and the many blessings they had received during their wanderings here on earth.

"Onkel Lehmann," Mutti said softly during one service, "the Lord has been so good to us. He has put it in your heart to take us all in, and we've already seen how safe we are here. I know that your years of faith in the Lord are benefiting us now. Thank you for taking me and my family into your home. We would be homeless without you and the Lord." Her voice was beginning to break as she continued, "When I accepted Jesus as my Saviour, as a young teenager, I never imagined what brothers and sisters in the Lord could mean to each other, in times of joy and in times of trouble. It always amazes me how the Lord chooses just the right person for a particular job—and no one could have filled your place better during the last few months.

"Sometimes I am ashamed, though, when I think how long I struggled against the Lord because I did not consider myself a sinner. I rebelled whenever I heard that the Bible says we are all sinners. I thought I was a good person—surely I would get to heaven. But one Easter Sunday I learned that Christ suffered and died for me personally. Then I knew that I could no longer bypass this Jesus. I, a sinner, prayed for the Lord to forgive me and come into my heart. I am so thankful! Jesus has been so faithful to me. That I am alive and speaking to you all is proof of His goodness. I hope and pray that all of you here will invite Jesus into your lives, if you have not already done so."

We spent the rest of our "service" in prayer. Everyone participated, and we all felt so close to God, having reason every day to thank Him for His protection. We asked Him to keep us safe during the night and the next day. Whenever I heard Onkel Lehmann pray, I thought he must be standing in the very throne room of God.

"Talking to God is like talking to your earthly father," Onkel Lehmann would tell us, "even though He is the Creator of the universe."

Another exciting part of our devotional time for me was the hymn-singing. No one sang out loud, of course. It was just a whispering choir because we didn't want to be heard by the Russians who were prowling outside. Everyone sang songs from memory. Many of the hymns were repeated daily, and after a short time we all learned new verses from each other.

One of the neighbor ladies who, with her four children, had been staying at our little farm since the day of our surrender, had been growing increasingly concerned about her father. He had been at work when she left with the children but she'd left a note. She slipped into her home several times daily, but discovered no trace of him. One day just as darkness set in while we were assembling for the mini-service, she returned in hysterics. "He is gone! He is dead! Why, God? Why? He is dead!"

Onkel Lehmann tried to comfort her and make some sense from her words, but she could only cry uncontrollably. Finally we were able to understand what she was saying.

"My father hanged himself in the attic! He is dead!"

Everyone was silent and stunned. Our wonderful neighbor committed suicide? I had so many unanswered questions, and I think the others did, too.

Our service that night was more of a funeral. For the first time since we lost our freedom everyone was weeping freely.

"Lord, we pray for this dear neighbor," Onkel Lehmann started, "and her young children. We are so saddened by the news concerning her father. Give this family the fortitude to stand alone now, and this lady wisdom until her husband is able to return to them. Comfort and guide them as only you can.

"And Lord, I also pray for the other women here who don't know where their husbands are. The Bible says You are concerned about every sparrow that falls and You know where the men, the fathers of these children, are. Guard and protect them, we ask, and draw us all close to You."

Seldom could we enjoy our services without interruptions by groups of Russians who searched the house and, with guns pointing at us, tried to intimidate us. That night's soldiers smelled filthy and could have been trailed through pitch darkness by the smell of liquor on their breath. We knew God was answering our prayers because they did us no harm.

For weeks the school across the road from us had been a home to some of the refugees from Eastern Germany. They had arrived there on foot, carrying a few bundles and pulling their children and old relatives on sleds and handcarts. One day we noticed they were filing past our windows in long, sad lines. We learned that they had been told to leave Lippehne. None of them knew where to go, but with tears and sadness, the homeless Germans trekked toward their unknown destination.

"Mommy, I want to sit in the wagon with Grandma," we heard a little girl beg.

"No, my dear! You are four years old and a big girl. This wagon is too heavy for me already. You must walk!"

"But where are we going, Mommy?"

"I don't know yet, child. We'll go to the end of this street and then we'll see."

When the last person from the school had passed our house, everything was quiet on the street. All the adults in our home were quiet, too. Onkel Lehmann broke the silence by saying, "Will we be next?"

Demanding knocks on the front door the next morning brought everyone to his feet with a jump. The knocking persisted, and Onkel Emil went to open the door. Two Russian officers told all of our friends and neighbors to leave. Only those who lived here could stay. With the enemies watching, the families gathered their belongings and began their rounds of teary good-byes. There was no time for a prayer, but I was sure that all those who remained behind whispered one for those who had to leave our place of safety.

Our service was very different that evening. No one felt like singing. The candle was lit, and Onkel Lehmann began to read Psalm 91:

> He that dwelleth in the secret place of the most High shall abide under the shadow of the Almighty. I will say of the Lord, He is my refuge and my fortress: my God; in him will I trust. Surely he shall deliver thee from the snare of fowler, and from the noisome pestilence. He shall cover thee with his feathers, and under his wings shalt thou trust: his truth shall be thy shield and buckler. Thou shalt not be afraid for the terror by night; nor for the arrow that flieth by day; Nor for the pestilence that walketh in darkness; nor for the destruction that wasteth at noonday.

"Then we skip down to verse 14." Onkel Lehmann continued,

> Because he hath set his love upon me, therefore will I deliver him: I will set him on high, because he hath known my name. He shall call upon me, and I will answer him: I will be with him in trouble; I will deliver him, and honour him. With long life will I satisfy him and show him my salvation.

After Udo blew out the candle, Onkel Emil, who had been the choir leader in Insterburg, couldn't resist the urge to sing. "God be with you till we meet again," he sang softly. No one else joined him.

Onkel Emil requested special prayer for his wife. She was supposed to meet him in Lippehne should the war separate them, but she had never come. He also requested prayer for his two grown daughters whose whereabouts were not known either. His only son had been killed a year earlier when his submarine was destroyed.

The next day, Mutti drew Dieter and me away from the other children. "You have no idea how difficult it is for me to ask this of you," Mutti said to us. "I have prayed much about it and have

26

received no other answer. You know that food has become very scarce for us. Onkel Lehmann still has a few potatoes left, but our bread flour is used up and I know you haven't had enough to eat in some time. I would like both of you to go to town to see if any of the stores are open. If they are, you can buy something to eat. Go to the grocery store and the bakery to see what you can find." Mutti then prayed with us and helped us get ready to leave.

Did Mutti notice that my heart felt as though it was about to escape my body from fear? We were supposed to go out on the street? That was where our enemies were! We hadn't left the house since the day we started out for the railroad station. Now we were to leave everyone here and go out alone? Dieter didn't seem to have any questions or doubts. In minutes he was bundled up to face the cold world.

On our way to the stores on Main Street, we noticed that most of the neighbors' houses were empty. Many windows were broken and the doors ajar. Furniture, clothes, and household items were scattered throughout the rooms. Upholstered chairs were slashed and the stuffing scattered everywhere. Family pictures were ripped up, slashed, and lying on the floor. Most of the abandoned, plundered homes resembled dark caves. Their owners' treasures and lives were ruined.

On Main Street, entrances to all of the stores were wide open. Refugees and elderly townspeople were searching through every box in the grocery store for food, but there was nothing edible left under the counters, in the side rooms, or anywhere else.

"No, I hadn't heard about the butcher's wife," the old lady told someone.

"Well, first she hanged her son in the smoke house and then she hanged herself."

It made me shudder as I heard these two women talk. A mother hanged her son? I couldn't fathom that! Would Mutti ever be capable of doing such a horrible thing? Absolutely not! Her faith in the Lord would keep her from committing such a crime. Her faith was too strong for her to become that despondent, wasn't it? But the women's chatter was going on.

"You already know that the train, which took off from the station with the Nazis before the Russians came, was completely wiped out by bombs, right?"

27

The train was bombed? O Lord, thank you! I found myself praying silently. You have watched over us more than we realized. All of those people were killed? We could have been on that train!

Finding no food to take home to Mutti, Dieter and I left the grocery store and continued on down the street. Passing the shoe store, we noticed boxes and shoes scattered outside on the sidewalk. Inside, people were shoving and grabbing and helping themselves to the footwear they needed. There was no clerk—just boxes of merchandise strewn everywhere. I decided to hunt for a pair of knee-high boots because my shoes had been pinching my toes for some time. Dieter and I searched for a long time and finally found two matching pairs, one for each of us. My excitement about having such wonderful boots made all my fears vanish. Suddenly it didn't matter that we were walking among our enemies. It saddened me, though, to see the bakery boarded up and to realize the disappointment it would be for Mutti when we returned without food.

On the way home I wondered if I, for the first time in my life, had stolen something. But there had been no clerk in the store, I reasoned, and the old ladies had said that German currency was no longer valid. The store was wide open, and I needed boots in this winter weather.

Still, everyone at home was shocked to see us return with merchandise for which we had not paid. The issue of our boots was debated back and forth among the adults. "You, Liane and Dieter, already know the Ten Commandments, right?" Mutti asked.

"Yes, Mutti," we said in unison.

"Then you also know that one of those commandments of the Lord says: 'Thou shalt not steal,' right?"

"I realize that, Mutti," I answered, "but I needed boots so badly and Dieter has no winter shoes either. It took us a long time to find matching pairs. People were just throwing the boxes and shoes around and there were no clerks at the store either."

"I know what you are trying to tell me, Schaefle! But nevertheless you were taking property that belonged to someone else. That is called stealing. We are in a war situation, but that does not change the Word of God. His commands always remain the same."

"But the shopkeeper was probably a Nazi."

"He must have been, Schaefle, because he had his business until the Russians moved in. Vati and I were forced to close our store in Insterburg when we refused to join the party. But that still doesn't give us the right to take his merchandise."

"Maybe Jesus wanted us to have these shoes and boots. There would not be any left by tomorrow," Dieter suggested with a serious look on his face.

Mutti was silent for a long time. We stood and waited for judgment to be passed. It seemed like an eternity before she finally spoke.

"If there were anyone for you to return those boots to, you had better believe that you would be doing so." Mutti paused and sighed, pulling us both to her for a hug and a kiss. "Dieter and Liane, you are not to enter those stores again. Do you understand?"

"Yes, Mutti." Our answers blended. We were sober then, but I was on top of the world for the rest of the day because of my wonderful new boots. I couldn't believe I had never really looked at Mutti before today. I couldn't fathom how beautiful she was. Her dark brown, naturally curly hair and her dreamy eyes must have been the reason Vati married her. He had always said he married her because she loved the Lord and music, and because she had a sense of humor. But I thought he also married her for her great beauty. When, at times, I saw the sadness in her eyes, I felt heartbroken that she and Vati hadn't seen each other in such a long time.

The following day, Mutti again sent Dieter and me out to search for food. At the town square Russian soldiers were draped over their tanks and trucks while they were eating and drinking. My mouth began to water when we saw them chewing on dark bread and sausage. We hadn't had bread in days.

Dieter slowly moved closer to a group of soldiers. He was the cutest seven-year-old, with his light blond hair resembling a dandelion gone to seed. The soldiers liked him immediately and motioned for him to come closer. One Russian, with a broad grin on his face, gave him the heel of his black, hard bread. His friendliness made me bolder. I stretched my cold hand toward them, but they simply ignored me. I thought it was because I was not pretty. We stayed around the group a little longer, hoping to get more bread, but none of them looked at us again.

Half frozen, we dashed home through the snow. Being away from our family wasn't as scary as on the first day, and it made me feel good to see Mutti so excited about that piece of bread. She used it to cook bread soup. Our potato supply in the basement dwindled quickly. Mutti and Kaetchen boiled them one day and fried them the next. Without salt, however, they no longer tasted as wonderful as they used to. The day Dieter and I found a block of red cattle salt at an abandoned farm was a day of rejoicing for us. Mutti and Kaetchen invented a new way to cook the potatoes: they fried them in salt.

After Onkel Lehmann had given thanks for our first meal of salt-fried potatoes, he said, "Just think how wonderful our God is! I don't know if I told you this, Kaetchen, but when my farmer friend brought my potatoes last fall, he rolled them from his wagon right into the basement through the chute, as he usually does. When he came into the house to present me with the bill, I was absolutely shocked. He had delivered double the amount I ordered. Since there was no way for me to carry all those potatoes out of the cellar by hand, I decided to keep them. Now, of course, we see God's wonderful provision in my friend's mistake, don't we?"

One sunny, spring-like day in March the front door was almost smashed in. Onkel Emil slowly limped to remove the barricade and open it the rest of the way. This gave the women time to hide.

"Woman! Woman! Where woman?" Three young soldiers hollered as they came running into the house. Mutti and her sister-in-law were just dashing across the courtyard to hide in the outhouse. Seeing them, the soldiers chased after them and in their haste flung open the door to the coal storage room instead of the one the ladies had entered. With that door being open, the outhouse door was completely covered.

"Woman! Where woman?" they yelled at Onkel Lehmann, who was repairing his handcart in the yard.

"I haven't seen the women," he told them. "I don't know."

From the kitchen window Kaetchen and I watched him trying to explain to the soldiers that he really had not seen the women because his back had been turned, but they didn't understand. One of the soldiers, in his rage, drew his sword and held it above the kneeling preacher. Instinctively I closed my eyes.

"Where woman? Where woman?" he continued yelling.

I looked again. Suddenly, as if turned away by an unseen hand, the soldier put the sword back in its sheath, turned around, and all three quietly left the property. With our hearts racing from fear, Kaetchen and I embraced.

"Thank you, Lord," she said, "for sparing my dad and protecting the women."

Mutti and her sister-in-law came trembling out of their hiding place, their faces white and tear stained.

"Onkel Lehmann, we thank you," Mutti said while squeezing his hand. "You almost had to give your life for us. From the outhouse we saw everything through a knothole in the door. I am so glad you did not know where we were hiding. The Lord must have struck both you and our enemies with blindness to show Himself mighty. Thank you, Onkel Lehmann, but I wish you wouldn't have to endure so much because of us."

In the days that followed, Dieter and I continued to go on our begging trips. My heart still raced when Mutti let us out of the door, but I was less fearful of our enemies now. There were other things, however, that troubled me. Every time we walked along the peaceful lakes, I began to tremble because I thought about the mother of whom we'd heard who pushed each of her four children—oldest to the youngest—into the icy lake and then took her own life by drowning. We saw bodies washing ashore. Some of them were men; some of them you couldn't tell anymore who they'd been, but there was no one to bury any of them. The water and the elements were their grave. Why was God so good to us? I always asked myself.

"Kaetchen! Kaetchen!" Mutti said excitedly and joyfully one morning with her eyes sparkling. "Emil is alive! I know he is alive! The Lord has given me assurance of that during the night. The father of my four children is alive! I can't tell you how thankful and happy I am. There is no doubt in my mind! We do have a wonderful Lord!"

"Yes," Kaetchen rejoiced, "we have a wonderful Lord. I am so happy for you, Emmy." She turned her head and began to weep, and I knew she was thinking of her own husband.

"Children! Liane, Dieter, Marlies, and Udo come here!" Mutti quickly gathered us around her. "We have a wonderful God! He never disappoints us! Even when everything around us looks hopeless, we can trust in Him. You all know that we have not heard from Vati in almost a year. We didn't know if he was alive. This morning, however, I can tell you that Vati is alive! He is alive and well! Our Lord Jesus told me that last night. He told me that some day we are all going to see Vati again. I don't know when that will be, but I know that God will keep His promise, and we'll be reunited. Isn't that wonderful?

"Vati will be so proud of you children, and he will be so surprised to see how you have grown. I know you don't get enough to eat anymore and your little tummies are empty so much of the time, but the Lord Jesus can overrule all of those problems and still let you grow big and strong. We must believe that. I think we should thank the Lord right now for His goodness to us and for telling us about Vati."

On the evening of this happy day, Mutti handed me a poem which she had written. "Schaefle, I'd like you to memorize this. It is for Vati's homecoming celebration."

Dieter and I spent a large part of each day scavenging for food, and, as a result, we were becoming well acquainted with Lippehne. We cut through this farm yard and that garden. We knew all the abandoned homes and farms. We knew where to find troops and where to gather wood and sticks for our fire. We knew where the ruins were, and we learned about the two sides of our enemies: we knew how they treated both children and adults. But one day Dieter and I learned something new.

In our haste to reach the troops camping outside of town, we cut across the cemetery for the first time. With its large trees, it had always seemed to be quite a dark place. On this warm, sunny winter day, however, the cemetery looked almost inviting.

"Why are the doors to these house-graves open?" Dieter asked.

"You mean the catacombs?"

"Yes, those houses there."

"I don't know."

"Look! The caskets are open, too. There are bones on the ground and two skulls there in the corner."

For a while we just stood there, gazing in disbelief.

"These are parts of people who were alive at one time, Dieter." When I thought about my statement, my body started going into a succession of chills. Bones of people all around us? We checked further and realized that all the catacombs were open and the bones scattered. Instead of going begging, we suddenly found ourselves running home as fast as our legs could carry us.

"Why are we running, Dieter?" I panted when I regained some control of my thoughts.

"I don't know why you are running, but I am scared!"

When we related what we had just seen to the family at home, Onkel Lehmann said sadly, "Yes, at work the other day, I heard about the vandalism at the cemetery. It proved that our enemies have no respect for the dead either. The catacombs and caskets are torn open because it is there that the Russians find treasures such as jewelry, gold watches, and gold teeth."

Everyone was shocked by this explanation. Mutti gave Dieter and me a hug and a kiss and tried to comfort our troubled minds. The next day, of course, we were out begging again.

A great number of soldiers had been camping outside the city gate for several days. As we approached them slowly, they immediately began paying attention to my cute brother. They were barbecuing piglets over a huge fire built with chopped-up German furniture. One group was already eating, and they were calling Dieter over to where they were. He took off like lightning as I tried to follow. It couldn't be true! Were they giving my brother a piglet's head? What would we do with that? When Dieter turned around, I knew that this was exactly what had happened. There was no way I could keep up with my brother now. He was running toward home with his treasure, faster than I had ever seen him run. In a few moments he had slipped into a side street and was out of my sight.

As I continued trying to catch up to Dieter, a Russian stepped into my way and told me to stop. He motioned for me to sit on a stone wall and take off my new boots. He then began to unlace his beat-up combat boots and pulled out his feet. As he began to unwrap the filthy rags which covered his bare feet, a nauseating stench filled the late winter air around us.

He then made me put my feet in his boots while he tried and tried again to squeeze his big feet into my beautiful boots. But no matter how hard he tried, they just wouldn't fit. My heart was racing, but at the same time I was rejoicing. I would never be able to walk home in his huge canoes. Shouting something

I didn't understand, he angrily threw my boots toward me. In no time at all my feet were back where they belonged. I wanted to start running away, but he grabbed me by the arm and took away my mittens that Omi had knitted for me. When he finally let me go, I wasted no time in leaving. Mutti was very glad to see me and gave me a big bear hug when I finally reached home. The piglet's head was already boiling in a pot of water on the stove. It turned out to be the most delicious soup we had eaten in a long time.

"Thank you, Lord," Onkel Lehmann prayed, "for again supplying our needs."

How we would survive without a regular means of getting food was the most important question now. Dieter and I continued to scrounge around town for anything edible. In our search we sometimes spent all day away from home. Our only hope was our enemies. They were vicious but had always been kind to us children.

When the Russian hospital, which had been housed in our old school, was evacuated, Dieter and I found many bread crusts under the beds and among the bloody bandages. We brought them home. Mutti scraped and washed off some of the dirt and cooked bread soup. The hospital yielded enough bread for several days of food for our family.

4
Enemy in the Camp

Not a day went by without a visit from our fur-hatted enemies whose demands never changed. All the ladies at our house continued to dress like scarecrows. The influx of the Cossacks always increased after 9:00 P.M., when the curfew for the Germans began. Then one day in the middle of the afternoon three clean-looking soldiers informed us that the ground floor of our little house had to be vacated. It was needed for officers immediately, and those living downstairs would have to join Mutti and the rest of us in our tiny quarters on the second floor.

"Your father soldier?" a tall officer with a grin on his face asked me in broken German.

"Yes," I answered. The Russian tilted his head, seeming to wait for a more specific answer.

"He is in France."

The same officer then followed me into the kitchen and inquired of my aunt if everyone in our house was healthy.

"Yes," she told him without hesitation.

Just before darkness fell, we were all trying to find a place to sleep in our small room. As usual, no one undressed. We had gone to bed fully dressed for weeks now. Sometimes I was too warm sleeping all bundled up under the down covers, but Mutti always insisted that we had to be prepared in case of an emergency. We'd freeze to death outside if we had to leave the house suddenly.

My aunt, Dieter, and I crowded onto the couch near the window. Some of the others settled down on the bed and the rest on the floor. No one in our group was sleeping, except for the little ones. Fear kept everyone else awake and quiet. Our enemies were in our house tonight.

Not a word was said, but tension was building in our room as if we were all in a pressure cooker. I could feel my aunt's heart pound even though I slept at her feet. Why did everything seem so frightening? Usually I felt safer when we were all together. I was listening into the darkness, but I didn't know what I expected to hear. Why had they forced all of us into one room? I couldn't find the answers.

My imagination, however, continued to show me all kinds of horrible pictures. I wanted to sleep, but I couldn't stop thinking. The moon was filtering its cool beams through the lace curtains and casting designs on Vilmar's face. He was sleeping so peacefully. Why couldn't I sleep like that? I was so tired.

Suddenly I heard thunder-like steps on the wooden staircase. The steps were moving upward, closer and closer, and then our door was kicked and pushed open. In the moonlight I saw a tall shadow.

"You sleep?" the voice asked harshly in German. Nobody answered. Two more footsteps and the door was being closed from the inside. In a very calm voice the man informed us in broken German that he was an officer. He had studied in St. Petersburg, Russia. His parents owned a business, and he had three beautiful sisters. All three of them had been raped by men of the German SS. He questioned us about our relationships to one another. Now I realized something. This was the same voice that had asked me where Vati was. I quietly let out a sigh of relief. This Russian had been nice to me. I liked his blue eyes and neat appearance. He seemed so different from the other Russians we had encountered. I knew he wouldn't harm us. I was sure.

All of a sudden, though, he started yelling at Onkel Emil. "Why not speak right, Father? You not father of children here.

Why not speak right, Father? Why?" Had Onkel Emil told him that he was our father? Why would he have done that?

"You not speak right. Why? Why?" And the officer raised his arm and shot into the ceiling with his pistol. Immediately all the little ones awakened and began to scream. He shot again and again. "You not speak right, Father. You not father!"

My ears were about to explode as he continued to shoot. In the middle of his spree of madness, the door flew open, and someone else burst into the room.

"Me do it alone!" he shouted and pushed the officer out the door. Yelling and hollering in Russian, the first visitor clumped downstairs.

The little ones continued to scream, and in the moonlight I saw Kaetchen and her two sons cowering in one corner of the room. The Russian moved over to her and ran both hands down her skinny body. "Nicht gut! Nicht gut!(Not good)" he grunted, and in the same manner began to size up Mutti. Marlies and Udo feverishly clung to her. That made him furious, and he turned away from her also. Mutti's beautiful sister-in-law quickly reached over the foot of the bed for Udo and used his little body to shield her face. The Russian now moved over to our couch. "You mother?" he asked my aunt.

"Yes," she answered, trembling.

"You, Dummkopf (dumbhead)," he shouted. "You not mother. Mother not holding child in face. Mother holding child close to heart." He grabbed Udo and shoved him back at Mutti. "You, Father," he yelled at Onkel Emil, "on floor! All on floor!" he commanded. Onkel Emil struggled to move quickly but the wooden leg slowed the process. The invalid moved too slowly for the beast that had found its prey. "On floor," the Russian hollered again and planted his pistol on Onkel Emil's forehead.

"Shoot us all!" Mutti intervened, placing her hand between Onkel Emil's head and the pistol. "Shoot us all! Just shoot us all!"

"No, no," he scoffed. "German woman go-o-o-o-d woman." The Russian, withdrawing his pistol, stumbled to the couch. I was still at my aunt's feet because there was no room left on the floor. With one hand he seized my aunt by the hair and stretched out next to us, pistol still in his other hand.

When daylight broke and I awakened, the rapist had left. I found myself on the floor near the couch. White billowy clouds, edged in light red, were moving slowly above the school building. My aunt was crying softly. Just a few months earlier, her husband, my uncle, had been killed while defending Insterburg. He had loved his beautiful, God-fearing wife dearly. The nightmare was over for the rest of us, but I felt it would never be over for her. As I lay quietly on the floor, I was counting the bullet holes in the ceiling. There were twenty-one.

We had no access to our kitchen that morning and everyone was hungry. How would we prepare our potato breakfast? The smell of fried bacon, which our enemies seemed to be enjoying, was trailing upstairs to our room, making us even hungrier. Were they matter-of-factly eating without realizing our plight? "One of us will have to go downstairs and request some food for the children," Mutti said boldly. But who would it be? That question was debated for some time. There was much to be considered, as no one was able to predict our enemies' dispositions. They could harm the petitioner or kill him, or harm the rest of us for even making such a request. We were completely at their mercy. Finally Kaetchen could no longer bear the suffering of her two-year-old.

"I will go," she said in her gentle voice, sighing deeply. "But you must all pray for me. God will have to perform another miracle today. We all know that we have a wonderful God. He can do anything to help His children, right?" She rose from the floor, straightened her black dress and smoothed her hair, which was twisted into a bun on the back of her head.

"Before you go, Kaetchen," Onkel Emil began, "I have to apologize to all of you for the problems I caused. I have already asked the Lord to forgive me for lying and telling the Russian that I was the father of Emmy's children. I lied thinking that I might be able to protect them. But as I considered everything this morning I realized that I just limited the Lord that way. He could have protected us without my sin of lying. All of these experiences are new to us, and I would never have imagined that I'd lie under pressure. This shows me that I have to move much closer to our Lord so it won't happen again. From now on I will be truthful with our enemies. Will you all please forgive me?"

"I forgive you," Kaetchen answered.

"I forgive you, too," more voices joined in.

"I have to ask for forgiveness, too," my aunt said between sobs. "I am so sorry that I used a little child in trying to protect myself. Please forgive me."

"We will."

Kaetchen quietly opened the door, slipped out, and closed it. The farther downstairs she walked the more bold and determined her steps sounded. A prayer meeting started immediately and seemed to last for a long time. Everyone was listening for her footsteps, but none could be heard. Why was she staying away so long? What was happening in the kitchen? Was she being molested? Would she ever come back? My mind was turning somersaults as it considered all these questions. Who would take care of Hanno and Vilmar should something happen to Kaetchen? Why? Why was it taking her so long? It was very difficult to continue listening for her footsteps because of the little ones' cries. All of a sudden Kaetchen bounced into the room.

"This is a day of sadness but also of rejoicing," the young preacher's wife announced to everyone in her bubbly way, with a sparkle in her brown eyes. "The Lord does not forget His own. All the children are invited to feast at the table of our enemies. Let's go, children," she said, clapping her hands. That included even me, but I couldn't believe it. I was supposed to go to our enemies after what happened last night?

"Let's not waste time." Kaetchen fussed at us. Quickly we all got up and started downstairs. One of the officers ran his hand through Dieter's curly hair as we filed past the men into the kitchen. He said something we didn't understand. Other Russians were standing with folded arms, watching us. One picked up Marlies, played with her blond curls, and talked to her. She just smiled back at him.

Kaetchen made herself right at home in her kitchen. She reached for the dishcloth and wiped the table, took dishes out of the cupboard, silverware out of the drawer, and seated the six of us, three at each side of the table. The chubby Russian chef placed a large bowl of noodles on the table.

"Now, children," Kaetchen said, "let us all pray and thank our wonderful Lord for His bountiful blessings." Every pair of hands, even Udo's, were folded, our eyes were shut, and our heads were bowed. Kaetchen did the same.

"Come, Lord Jesus, be our guest and bless what You have given us. Amen," we all prayed in unison. When I raised my head, I realized that all the officers, about ten of them, and the cook were watching us. Was this really true? Did I see tears in the eyes of several of the Russians?

What a feast! Noodles! Even as they were sliding down my throat I still couldn't believe it. This must be a dream. As I felt my stomach filling up, I reasoned that it wasn't a dream because for the first time in I didn't know how long, my body seemed satisfied.

All the officers were standing near the table watching us silently devour the meal they had provided. When we were almost finished, one of them stepped closer to the table and handed each of us a chocolate bar. This had to be a dream. Noodles and a chocolate bar? Marlies was so excited that she went from one Russian to another to shake hands with each and say, "Danke schoen. Danke schoen. Danke schoen." One of them picked her up again and played with her while Kaetchen and I did the dishes. After we all thanked everyone, we scrambled upstairs with full tummies and chocolate bars in our hands.

"Mutti, Mutti," Dieter called and pushed the door open. "We ate noodles, real noodles."

"My tummy is full of noodles, too," Marlies added. "I like the Russians downstairs. Can I go down and play with them?"

"No, my little daughter. You just stay here now with the rest of us."

It was difficult for everyone in our room to believe what had just transpired in the kitchen. "God's Word never fails," Mutti remarked with tears in her eyes, realizing that our hunger pains had been stilled for the first time in several months. "We have experienced today what Psalm 23 really means: 'Thou preparest a table before me in the presence of mine enemies.' I just can't fathom how God's Word becomes more wonderful in these difficult days."

Around noontime the rapist returned to our house. Half-drunk and red faced, he stumbled into our room, approached my aunt, and handed her a loaf of bread and a chocolate bar. With tears cascading down her rosy cheeks she took both gifts and threw them at him. She turned away from him and continued to weep bitterly. He tried to put his arm around her, but she pushed him away. Her anger seemed to surprise him. He picked up the bread and chocolate and staggered out of the house, holding onto the walls.

Kaetchen was going downstairs again to ask for some drinking water. We were impatiently waiting for her. Finally she entered the room, totally out of breath. "When I knocked on the kitchen door to ask for water the cook slowly opened it and asked me in. Then he said slyly, 'Me do you favor, now you do me favor.' I knew immediately what he meant, took my bucket, and raced out of the kitchen. That man expected to be rewarded for his earlier translating efforts. He seemed like such a nice man. Of all the men in the kitchen, I felt he was the one who could be trusted. But we can't trust man. No wonder the Bible says, 'Trust in the Lord with all thine heart.' "

Later in the afternoon we heard trucks driving up to our house. Men yelled, hollered, and appeared to be joking downstairs and in the hallway. After the vehicles drove off, everything was quiet below us and remained so until Onkel Emil decided to go down to check on things. He found the front door wide open. The only traces of our "guests" were a dirty kitchen and a disorderly house. A search for food they might have left behind yielded nothing. Happy that we were alone again, Kaetchen and the others reoccupied the ground floor. But while everyone felt like celebrating, my aunt wept bitterly. Her beautiful face looked drawn, and her eyes were red and without a sparkle. Mutti and Kaetchen spent a considerable amount of time trying to comfort her, but their efforts were in vain.

Darkness found both mothers still cleaning the house, changing the linens, and scrubbing the greasy stove. Our small supply of firewood had dwindled remarkably while we had visitors.

"Schaefle, please bundle up your brothers and sister a little more," said Mutti. "Our firewood is almost gone and none of us have sufficient body fuel to keep warm."

"I will, Mutti. And don't worry. Dieter and I will go and gather sticks again tomorrow."

5
Scavengers

Dieter and I combed through houses and farms more diligently than ever. We had overcome all fear. We even searched garden cottages for edibles now, but found that all of them had already been ransacked. How beautiful the outer shells of the cottages were! Each one had its own personality, no doubt that of the former owner. Some of them were large with elaborate wooden trims, others were plain and unassuming. All of them had one feature in common, however: a wooden dock stretching into the open lake. A boat was usually tucked into the reeds next to the dock. Onkel Lehmann's big garden was located just a short distance from the former public beach and the large beach restaurant. His smaller garden was closer to his home at another lake.

Our potato supply had given out the week before. Ever since, everyone had besought the Lord for another miracle. Once again, He did not fail us.

"Dieter! Dieter! Look at this! Potatoes! We have found potatoes!"

"Are they still good? They look soft and mushy."

"Let's check and see. Yes, some of them are rotten, but most of them are still firm and good. We just have to sort them out."

"All right, sister. You can sort them out. I don't like to touch the soft ones. What made you look here behind this barn anyway?"

"I think that you should ask: 'Who made you look here?' "

"Well, then, who?"

"It must have been the Lord. He wanted us to find this cache. I would never have scrounged around back here on my own. So this is our miracle day—the day we have been waiting for! Let's look in the barn to see if we can find a bucket or something so that we can carry some of these potatoes home."

"The Lord be praised! Another miracle!" These were the expressions with which we were greeted at home. For days Dieter and I carried bucket after bucket of potatoes home, and the rejoicing didn't cease. Mutti, especially, was glad because she felt that the potatoes would help with some of the ill-effects we had been experiencing recently because of our poor diet.

"Perhaps the vitamins from these potatoes will start the healing of your legs, Dieter," Mutti said to him. "Are any of the boils opening yet?"

"Yes, they are. White stuff is coming out of them."

"Push up your pants legs and let me see. Oh no, my son! I didn't realize they have worsened so much in the past few days. We'll have to cut some bandages and start wrapping your legs."

"Can't we do that later? I want to get some more potatoes with Liane."

"No, we had better do it right now. Let's wash your boils in salt water first. I think the red cattle salt will probably work as well as the table salt that we don't have. Are your boils hurting yet, Dieter?"

"Yes, Mutti, they are, but I am strong, you know. I want to be like Vati. And he wouldn't complain."

"That is wonderful, my son. But I know they hurt because I have quite a few on my own arms and legs. Our bodies need vitamins from good food to help heal our festering skin. But you know, our Lord Jesus can heal this skin. And we'll trust Him that He will. In the meantime, though, we have to do everything we can to keep the sores clean. I will heat some water for you, and then we'll get started."

Mutti taught my poor brother how to bandage his legs, tie the bandages, and take off the soiled ones.

"Tomorrow," she said, "I will show you how to wash your bandages and roll them."

The next morning soldiers again beat on the front door, but for some reason seemed to wait patiently until Onkel Emil hobbled to open it. Through a German interpreter, they told us that they needed laborers. Walking down the long hallway, they turned into the kitchen where the rest of our group were busying themselves. Their first choice was Kaetchen. "You come," one said pointing to her. "You rabota (work). We will give bread."

Didn't they see how frail she was? I wondered. She weighed only about ninety pounds. They continued to insist that she go with them.

"My daughter has to stay here with her two young sons," Onkel Lehmann said boldly. "They need their mother. I will come and work for you."

"No, we need woman."

"Please take me instead," he begged.

Kaetchen's two sons clung to her. "Stay here, please, Mutti!" Five-year-old Hanno looked at the soldiers and continued his plea. "Do not take our Mutti away." They were visibly surprised.

"You come, man," the leader motioned and began to pull Onkel Lehmann by the arm. "And you, too, woman," another said to my aunt as he started dragging her out of the house. Mutti quickly reached for my aunt's coat and tossed it to her.

"We'll pray," she called over the shoulder of one Russian.

Both workers returned home in the evening totally exhausted. "They have no respect for their own dead," Mutti's sister-in-law grumbled. "No respect. First they buried their comrades in the town square, and then we had to dig them up and move them to another place. The stench was unbearable. Some Germans passed out. Because the sick ones failed to meet their work quota, the rest of us had to work extra hard. I didn't get the promised bread either. I wish that Russian would have shot me the other night. How much more do we have to endure? Is God forsaking us?"

There was total silence in the room. Did my aunt really mean what she said?

"I had to bury cadavers all day long," Onkel Lehmann reported. "Apparently when the soldiers are hungry they shoot domestic animals at random. They cut out a piece of meat to roast and let the rest of it spoil. Cadavers are scattered all around town.

Two other old men and I had to dig holes and bury those stinking, rotting animals. They kept their word to me, though, and gave me a piece of bread. It is black and hard, see? But if you soak it, Kaetchen, I think you can probably make some good soup from it. I also have another surprise for everybody," he continued joyfully. "I have the inner organs of a calf—one shot probably just this morning—here in my shirt. I had no other way to bring my treasure home. Can you imagine what wonderful soup we can make from this?"

Onkel Lehmann was right. The soup was delicious. The inner organs of an animal, that none of us had ever eaten before, really eased our hunger pangs.

"The small farmhouse is simply too crowded for all of us," my aunt announced one day. "Omi and I have decided to move back across the street, now that things have become some-what calmer. If we move, the rest of you will have a little more room here."

"But will you be all right over there all by yourselves?" Mutti asked. "The people you were staying with are gone now, you know."

"Yes, I know, but we'll be just fine."

The thought of my aunt and Omi leaving depressed me. I was going to miss both of them, but especially Omi. She was such a sweet and wonderful little lady. She always wore a long, black dress and a dark apron, which covered most of the front of her dress. Her gray hair was pulled back into a bun, and the smile seldom left her face. I loved her dearly, and I knew she loved us children very much.

In Insterburg she and Opi (Grandpa) always did special things for us grandchildren. They even planted a fruit tree in their garden for each of us. I could hardly wait until the end of summer when I could harvest the egg-sized yellow plums from my own tree. Because most of the trees in their garden were uncommon, friends, neighbors, and even strangers came to admire them. One of their apple trees bore apples the size of a child's head.

Whenever we went to my grandparents' house, Opi would sit in his workshop on the cobbler's bench, repairing saddles and tack for the farmers. In the summer Omi kept busy in the large garden, picking fruit and vegetables and preserving them. But the thing Omi liked best was to beat fresh eggs with sugar and serve us a bowl of it every time we visited. Dieter and I took that two-mile walk to our grandparents' at least twice a week. It was always such an exciting place to be.

Many evenings we would go to their house, especially when Vati was home from the service. Sitting in the living room, we would sing hymns, read the Bible, and pray. Opi's long, white beard and snow-white hair always made me visualize how the old Bible patriarchs must have looked. Opi and Vati used to take turns playing the pump organ. How I missed Opi! I was glad, though, that he had gone to heaven just three months before we all had to leave Insterburg and thus was spared being a witness to the destruction of his beloved city.

It sometimes broke my heart now to see Omi getting more frail. Dieter and I visited her often and usually found her sitting at the window reading her Bible. When we took some potatoes to her she was always thrilled. Sometimes she grated them for pancakes, but before the pancakes were baked, she let the grated mixture stand in a bowl for several hours in order for the starch to settle on the bottom. Then she poured off the batter and the sediment, starch, was left in the bowl. The starch was dried in the sun to be used as flour for baking or for making pudding.

"Look at this, Liane! Look! Look what I found!" Dieter exclaimed one day while we were out hunting for food. He began bubbling with joy as we turned a street corner. "Look! There's something I have always wanted. A bike! What would a bike be doing here in the middle of the street, except waiting for me?" My happy brother reached down to raise it up.

"But Dieter! This bike has only metal rims! It has no rubber tires! You can't ride that on the cobblestones!"

"I can on the sidewalks. Just watch me!" And suddenly the empty street was filled with the noise of a tireless bike clanking down the sidewalk. Every seam in the large stone blocks accentuated the clatter as the metal rims rambled down the Luisenstrasse. Dieter was too short to sit on his new treasure. He had to ride it standing up.

Should I go begging alone, I wondered? Or should I wait for my brother, who apparently had no hunger pangs at all today?

I decided to wait, hoping he would tire of his new toy soon; but instead he continued to ride up and down our street. Then, suddenly, his world crashed in. A Russian approached him and told him to stop, just as he was trying to zip past me. Mumbling something we didn't understand, the soldier grabbed Dieter's bike with his right hand. But why did the soldier need this old bike when he held onto a brand-new one with his left hand? He mumbled again and shoved the new bike toward Dieter. My brother took it, jumped on, and in total silence started peddling to the next street and around the block.

The Russian made many attempts to ride the old piece of junk but was unsuccessful. Weaving back and forth as if he were drunk, he fell off again and again. It was so funny to watch this clumsy man. His snow-white teeth sparkled as he talked to himself, but I noticed he was becoming increasingly angry. I decided it was best for me to leave, yet I watched him out of the corner of my eye. Furiously he kicked the bike several times with his filthy boots before he started to push it up the street. I hoped Dieter wouldn't appear around the corner. He would definitely lose his bike. This man had changed into a mad dog.

"Can you imagine, sister, that I have a bike?" When Dieter rejoined me, he couldn't be quieted. "My own bike! I can't believe that he is so stupid. It is so easy to ride a bike—and nobody is going to get this new bike from me, either! I stopped before turning the street corners and checked for soldiers. Do you know that I watched the Russian fall off this bike, too, when I was riding past him on the old piece of metal?" Both of us were now standing in the middle of the street laughing so hard that I thought my cheeks would burst.

When we showed Dieter's treasure to everyone at home, no one seemed to be able to believe the story. I noticed Mutti, however, looking up as if she was thanking the Lord for making her son's dream come true.

"I am so happy for you, my son. You go and ride your bike for awhile. You can go begging later," Mutti suggested.

"Thanks, Mutti," he said hurriedly. Dieter rushed outside and we all watched him zip around the corner of the house with lightning speed.

I had a good time for a while, entertaining Marlies and Udo. I hadn't been able to spend much time with them lately, and it was hard to realize how quickly they were growing up. Udo got along beautifully with his sister, and she in turn with him.

"Dieter! Dieter!" Udo suddenly interrupted our game.

"Dieter isn't here, Udo. He is riding his bike."

Then I saw Dieter myself.

"He took my new bike. My brand-new bike," he sobbed, rushing up the stairs, his dusty face tear-stained and his eyes red. "He just came out of a house when I was riding by and told me to get off. And then the Russian took it. He just took my new bike and chased me away. I want my bike back, Mutti, my new bike," he cried bitterly.

"A Russian surprised you and took your bike?"

"Yes, he did."

"I am so sorry, my son. I wish you could have kept that bike forever, but at least you had it for a little while. The Lord can give you a new bike again some day, Dieter. You know that He can do anything, right? He has proven that today, hasn't He?"

"But why couldn't He let me keep my bike, Mutti?"

"I don't know the answer to that question, Son. But I know for certain that someday you will have a bike that you can keep. I have been praying for that, and I will continue to do so. I know you are hurting terribly now, but that hurt will leave and you will feel better soon. Why don't we thank the Lord Jesus for the wonderful time you did have today with a brand-new bike and ask Him right now for another one."

"Yes, Mutti, let's do that. I know that Jesus can do anything."

Mutti and Kaetchen spent much of their time caring for the children, scrubbing the laundry on the washboard, and keeping the house in order. Whenever I was at home, I helped them. I did the darning, and it took up a lot of my time since the war-time socks seemed to fall apart after every wash.

"Pull the sock nice and taut over the darning mushroom," Mutti instructed me. "Stitch the darning yarn across the hole in a nice square or rectangle. Don't pull it too tightly. When you start weaving the needle up and down over the cross threads, make sure you weave a nice, flat patch. If anything puckers, it will hurt the foot when you wear shoes."

As soon as I had mastered the first few darning lessons, I spent many hours a week on my assignment. I had to darn socks for eleven feet. Since Onkel Emil had elevated himself as guardian

49

and protector of our family and had no one but us to care for him, I had to darn his socks, too. His were the ones I really dreaded darning because they always had the largest holes. I presumed that must have been due to the fact that his whole body weight rested on one leg. Darning his socks was almost as bad as having to wash my youngest brother's soaked pants every day. Because rubber pants were no longer available, he had to wear woolen pants, which Omi knitted for him, and they had become like felt from their constant use.

I considered my lot easy, though, when I compared it to Mutti's work. She was now stitching fur coats for the Russians by hand. Several officers saw her sewing one day and a short time later returned with furs to make long coats for their wives. Mutti sat all day now and sewed; at night she stitched by candlelight. Her fingers were often bleeding from the difficult work, but how she rejoiced when she received an occasional payment: a loaf of black bread.

New troops moved into Lippehne every few days, and it was always during the night hours that our visitors stomped through the house and yard in search of German soldiers. The hay, which they continually pierced with their swords or bayonets, was strewn all over the barn. No one would be able to survive under that hay, should he choose to hide there. In spite of the constant danger that still lurked about us, especially at night, Kaetchen and Mutti became happier and more confident.

"Emmy," Kaetchen remarked one day while she was upstairs visiting us. "Wouldn't our lives be barren without all of these experiences the Lord sends our way? Miracle upon miracle every day! The greatest one is that we are still alive. I just marvel at the grace of God every day when I hear the shooting outside and see the wooden hearses being pulled past our house."

"We don't deserve it," Mutti replied. "God is so faithful in answering our prayers. If we knew what the future held, we might despair. But we know He is in control. He has the answers to all of our questions. He knows how we will feed our six children. He knows where our husbands are. He also knows if we will pass the tests He gives us. We must continue to plant our faith firmly in Him!"

"Mutti, my head hurts," Marlies interrupted the conversation.

"Did you bump your head somewhere, Pittimaus?"

"I don't know, but it hurts all over. I want to scratch all the time. Will my hair fall out if I do that?"

"Oh no, Pittimaus. Your hair will not fall out if you do that. Let's go to the window where we have more light, and I'll look at your head." With the sun beaming through the small roof window, Mutti immediately detected the problem.

"Lice! I have never seen any before! But from what I have heard, this fits the description. Where could Marlies get lice?" Mutti asked Kaetchen. "The house is clean. The linens are scrubbed and boiled. Do you think someone else has them? The children play together all the time. Have your sons complained about anything?"

"No, they haven't. But I will check immediately," Kaetchen answered with concern in her voice.

"Kaetchen, I think I have the answer," Mutti whispered, leaning over the banister. "Marlies got the lice from the Russians. You know how fearless she is, climbing on their laps when any one of them sits down, and they always pick her up, too, and play with her blond curls. I think that is our explanation."

"You may be right, Emmy."

A thorough check of the house revealed no lice anywhere, except on Marlies' pillow. Mutti immediately began to delouse the little wiggleworm who sat on her lap playing with wooden beads. The sunlight was a blessing that day especially, with this painstaking task.

Fortunately, not too many of the small visitors had invaded yet. With a lot of patience, searching, washing, and scrubbing, Mutti was able to win the battle against the lice within just a few days.

"The neighbor across the street knows how to swim with the tide," Mutti remarked to Kaetchen one dreary morning in March. "There is a steady stream of Russians going in and out at her place. It must be because she can converse with them in Russian. There must be some reason, though, for her lacking nothing. Don't you think so, Kaetchen? Why is she so friendly with the enemy? Could she possibly be an informer?"

Mutti and Kaetchen strained their minds, trying to analyze the actions of the lady. The other day when she had come across the street for the first time since the invasion, she had seemed as kind as ever. She'd even brought us a bunch of carrots. How

51

could she be a friend of both the enemies and the Germans? Both Mutti and Kaetchen really wrestled with that question.

One day, shortly thereafter, the soldiers were looking for workers again. "You come! You come!" one of them shouted at Kaetchen and pulled her away from the scrubbing board. Hanno and Vilmar tried to hold on to their mother, but the soldier pushed them aside and dragged her by the arm along the hallway. Kaetchen was too physically weak to resist and had no choice but to go along. She was not dressed warmly either, but was not permitted to get a coat.

"We will pray for you," Mutti called as Kaetchen was pushed out the front door. Sadness gripped my heart, and I realized that my concern for Kaetchen was growing. Mutti called a prayer meeting, and after we had finished pleading for protection for her, my soul rested in the knowledge that Kaetchen was truly safe in the arms of Jesus.

"Schaefle, can you imagine that the Lord prepared me for this time many years ago?" Mutti asked as I watched her begin her fur sewing. She was carefully folding back the little animal hairs with her needle. "You see, if I had not learned this when I took tailoring lessons as a teenager, I wouldn't know how to sew fur seams invisibly. It just amazes me," she continued, "how wonderfully our Heavenly Father cares for us, even while we are young, teaching us lessons that we can draw on later in life."

"My mother always used to say to my sister and me: 'A girl has to be able to do everything.' And I am so glad she made that a slogan. I did learn so much when I was young. Besides the fact that many of the skills I gained are pleasurable, they have helped me so much in life. How barren my life would be if I didn't know how to cook, bake, sew, knit, crochet, embroider, and do garden and farm work. As I think of these things, I wish I had more time to fulfill my obligation to the new generation, you and Marlies. You have had to learn many things fast, my Schaefle, during the past few months. I just wish I had the time to teach you more. Perhaps some day I won't be so busy. I am really pleased, though, with the excellent job you are doing in darning the socks."

"Thank you, Mutti. But I don't like to darn. Knitting and crocheting are more exciting to me. Do you know that I have been crocheting for six years already?"

"Yes, I am aware of that. That field is inexhaustible, however.

You need to become more proficient in knitting, too. That green and yellow pleated skirt you knitted for the large doll, should have, I think, a yoked popcorn-stitch ski sweater to match, don't you think so? When the days lengthen, and I have finished my orders, I will teach you that knitting technique, all right? I should have some time in another week."

"I can't wait, Mutti. I can't wait."

Several hours after Kaetchen had left with the soldiers, someone knocked on the downstairs bedroom window. Hanno rushed to the front door and called, "Mutti! Mutti! Liane, please open the door. Mutti is outside!"

"Please calm down, Hanno. How do you know that?"

"I saw her through the window."

After assuring myself that it was indeed Kaetchen, I opened the door. Mutti had left her sewing to check on all the commotion in the hallway.

"Kaetchen, what happened to you? You are as white as a sheet," Mutti remarked. "Why are you out of breath? Are you all right?" Kaetchen leaned against the hallway wall as tears uncontrollably rushed down her face and onto the heads of her sons. Both of them had their arms slung around her tiny waist. Her dark dress was wet in the knee area, and her hair untidy. She was incapable of talking as she continued to sob and tremble. All of us stood in total silence.

"Our very lives are at stake." Kaetchen finally broke the silence with a quivering voice. "Our nation cannot survive this tyranny. The Russians want us dead. They are going to kill us all, one way or another." She faded into a breathless pause.

"They herded about sixty women into the school across the street. They had to clean up the mess the hospital left behind, scrubbing walls and floors, while the soldiers beat them with their guns if they didn't work fast enough. Many of the women have bleeding hands and are exhausted. I worked with them for a while. During some of this time we could hear screaming from somewhere nearby. There was no time to wonder about that, though because soon I was marched to another building and pushed into a long, very narrow room."

" 'Daway rabotay (get to work), woman!' the young Russian commanded as he shoved me with his gun. 'You scrub walls!' Then he left."

"After my eyes got used to the dim light, I was about to begin. But suddenly I began to shudder. 'Can this be true?' I was thinking. 'Are these walls splattered with fresh blood? Is this the blood of those we heard screaming? Where are they now? Are they alive or dead?' My body began to tremble at these thoughts, and I knew I had to get out. But how could I escape without getting shot? The huge school yard was filled with Russians guarding the workers. 'Please, Lord, help,' I whispered and immediately felt strength surging through my body. Leaving the room, I started walking across the school yard with all the Russians watching me, including the one who had pushed me into that bloody room. Nobody stopped me. They all stared straight at me—through me—as I walked past them and out through the gate. And here I am!" Her dark eyes were moist and sparkling as she continued, "Our God is real! He is real! He is the same God who delivered Daniel out of the lion's den. He must have blinded my enemies so that they could not see me walk across the school yard. If they had seen me, they would definitely have shot me. Oh, children! What would we do without the Lord?"

With that question lingering in the hallway, the little ones began to play again, and Mutti and Kaetchen talked quietly until Onkel Lehmann returned home from work.

6
The Eye of
the Storm

Early the next morning, someone beat violently on the front door. When Onkel Emil opened it, a Russian said in broken German, "You all out! All out of house! Officers need house. Out right now!"

"Do you mean you want us to vacate the house? For how long?"

"Not know. Need house right now," he repeated rather impatiently. "All out! Out now!"

"We need a little time," Onkel Emil pleaded. "Need place to go. You give us thirty minutes to move?"

"No! You out fifteen minutes!" and the spokesman and his two buddies planted themselves in the hallway and waited.

"I'll quickly go to the home of two of our elderly church ladies to see if we can move in with them," Onkel Lehmann suggested. He was on his way out as he spoke.

"Schaefle, check your rucksack quickly and add a few more clothes, your most important clothes. Then please dress Marlies and Udo warmly while I gather some of the other things we need," Mutti told me, words tumbling out of her mouth as quickly as water rushes through rapids.

Completely out of breath, Onkel Lehmann returned with good news: "We are welcome at the home of the two seamstresses. These two Christians didn't even hesitate to invite the ten of us into their home. Praise the Lord."

The rest of us raced here and there, grabbing this and reaching for that.

"The handwagon is ready," Onkel Emil called. "Bring your bundles."

Dieter and Onkel Lehmann squeezed past the Russians with our luggage and rushed into the yard. Hurriedly we threw things into the wagon while Onkel Lehmann worked feverishly to organize them so that no space would be lost.

"Out! Out! Fast!" the spokesman shouted, becoming very impatient. "We not take things. You come back. Officers good to Germans." One of the men stomped up the curved staircase to our living quarters. He saw Mutti's Bible on the table of our room.

"You read Bible?" he asked Mutti with a twinkle in his eyes.

"Yes, I do."

"Me too," he told us. "You not worry. Not take things. Not worry." He clogged downstairs again.

Udo and Vilmar were seated on top of the bundles as Onkel Lehmann opened the little shed door that led to the street. The handwagon rumbled across the cobblestones as he and Mutti pulled it. It wasn't easy for Kaetchen and me to help steady the little ones while carrying bundles and fighting the cold wind that whipped our faces on this sad March morning. As we struggled uphill on the next street, we could already see the white stucco house of the two sisters.

They were lovely ladies, and I was excited about seeing them again. After our boat rides last year, they often invited us to their house for cake and coffee. Their yeast cakes, topped with fruit and streusel, were always delicious, and we children were served plenty of milk. As we trudged up the hill I thought, "Why, why, why do I always think about food when I know that my caved-in and empty stomach hurts even more then? When will I finally learn not to dwell on thoughts of food?"

It was a miracle; the two little ones weren't crying. They actually seemed to be enjoying the cold, fresh air and their ride on top of the bundles. They were taking an interest in everything:

houses, clouds chasing each other, and two Russians walking down the other side of the street.

After arriving at the sisters' home, we opened the huge door and entered into a passageway that ran under their house and into a small backyard. Quietly we all stood there while Kaetchen went up the staircase to their living quarters. Dieter immediately set out to explore. He would have loved to spend more time in the yard and investigate the many doors there, but with danger lurking everywhere, Mutti called him back.

"Look at this, Mutti," he said excitedly. "When this huge passage door is open, it completely covers the little red door up there. That's neat, isn't it?"

Mutti looked at the small door at the top of another, shorter set of steps and nodded her head. It seemed to me as though she were acting mechanically, as though her mind and thoughts were far from us.

"I wonder what is behind it." Dieter's curiosity was unsubdued. "Can I walk up those few steps and see?"

"Yes, Dieter." We hadn't heard one of the sisters coming down the stairs until she spoke. "That is where you and your family will live. There will not be room for all of you in there, so Kaetchen and her family will have to come upstairs with us. Here is the key to the door. Go and see how you like your new home."

I followed close behind as Dieter climbed up the wooden steps. He pushed the long metal key into the keyhole, turned it, and pulled down the large door handle. The door fell open and Dieter shouted with excitement, "Mutti, come and see this cozy little place!"

Mutti carried Udo up the steps into our new home.

"This is so small," Dieter continued. "Where will we all sleep?"

"We'll all sleep there in the bedroom," she answered and began to check through the kitchen.

"I'll sleep here in the kitchen," Onkel Emil's voice thundered. None of us had heard him coming and we all jumped. "I will not leave you here alone. That is too dangerous, especially at night. I will protect my family. Onkel Lehmann will take care of Kaetchen, and I will take care of all of you now that we have to split up."

I liked Onkel Emil, often feeling sorry for him when he talked about his wife and two daughters, but I resented it when he called us "his" family. I had to admit that he had protected us many times in the past few months, but when he spanked Dieter for practically no reason I hurt, too. Mutti always interceded for us, telling him that we were not his children, therefore he had no right to discipline us. He seemed to feel, though, that he had to help Mutti in Vati's absence.

Kaetchen and Onkel Lehmann lifted their bundles off the wagon, took the boys, and moved upstairs with the sisters. After our belongings were taken off, we pulled the wagon into the courtyard. I didn't remember ever having seen handwagons in Insterburg. They resembled miniature haywagons with four closed sides five to six feet long and two feet deep. The rims of the four wooden, spoked wheels were covered with a metal band. The axle and the handle bar were also made of wood. It seemed that everyone in Lippehne had such a wagon to transport hundreds of different items.

Our small, furnished apartment was cold even though we were bundled up. Only a few pieces of firewood were left at the stove. "Dieter and I will go and gather some firewood, Mutti, all right?" I asked. "It was quite windy last night, and there should be some sticks at the promenade."

"Thank you, Schaefle. You are thoughtful and helpful. Before you leave, though," Mutti told us, "we have to make some plans for our safety. You see, our new home is located only a few buildings from the main road that leads to Berlin. That means many troops are constantly passing through Lippehne just a few houses from us. That makes it far less safe here for us. We also live only a short distance from the town square, and you have told me that the square is always crowded with Russians. Living here is much more dangerous than it was at Onkel Lehmann's farm. So we have to take certain precautions. If nobody finds us here, we can be as safe as Noah was in the ark. But if we are careless, it could be the end for us."

"Your mother is absolutely right, children," Onkel Emil added. "This location is terribly dangerous. We are really at the mercy of the enemy here if they find us. We have no basement to hide in, no barn, no outhouse, and no shed. We are an open target for the Russians. The Lord can protect us here too, as

He has so miraculously done at the farm, but we have to do our utmost not to give away our hideout."

"We all have to be very quiet from now on," Mutti continued, "so we will not be detected. When you two leave the house to go begging, we will first check the street for soldiers without touching the curtains. We will also open the door very quietly, a crack at first, and listen for sounds in the passageway. Then we will peek, and if no one is in sight, you two will tiptoe down the steps. Should someone watch you when you return, don't come toward our home. Don't make any moves toward our door if a Russian is nearby."

"We understand, Mutti," Dieter said very somberly. "We'll be careful."

Onkel Emil went to the window that overlooked the street. "Coast is clear," he whispered.

Mutti cracked the apartment door, listened, and then opened it a little more. She kissed Dieter and me and said, "The Lord keep you," as we carefully moved down the steps.

Our walk to the lake was considerably longer from our new home. We were thrilled to see that a lot of dead wood had fallen out of the trees during the past windy night, and nobody had beaten us to it this morning. We had no problem filling our arms, but it was much more difficult to carry our loads home because of the distance. After delivering the wood, we went on a begging tour. The only place we found Russians eating today was at the town square.

"Look at that, Liane," Dieter said with a big grin on his round face. "A motorcycle! Every man's dream."

"You are not a man yet, little brother."

"But I'm dreaming! I wonder what it is like to ride a motorcycle," Dieter mused.

"I wouldn't know. I have never been on one, but did you know that Vati had a motorcycle when he was courting Mutti? He always traveled from Insterburg to Memel on it to see her."

"No, I didn't know that. I just know about our Olympia car, the one with the colored rings in the front, that the SS took from our garage. Do you think they would have taken it if Vati had been home?"

"Yes, they would have. They had orders to take our car whether Vati was there or not. They told Mutti not to be upset about losing the car. We would lose a lot more, they said. And they were right about that."

While we stood on the sidewalk and talked, the motorcyclist suddenly stopped in front of us. The smiling Russian pointed to Dieter and the back seat and motioned for him to jump on. In a split second my brother had hopped on and slung his short arms around the Russian's waist. Then the pair took off, riding in huge circles in the square. The Russian hollered at his buddies and grinned constantly. Dieter's smile was almost touching his ears. He was so happy. His dream had come true. After many dizzying loops around the square, his friend stopped and they both got off. Then the soldier motioned for Dieter to wait while he climbed onto the tank and vanished inside. A few moments later he reappeared, and I couldn't believe what I saw. He ran his fingers through Dieter's curls, smiled at him, and gave him a whole loaf of black bread. Dieter shook hands with his friend and dashed toward me. "This is heavy," he exclaimed proudly. "Here! Lift it!"

"It certainly is. It seems to be heavier than a five-pound loaf of German bread."

"What do you think Mutti will say when she sees this?"

"She'll be happy, Dieter."

I was glad for the food, but just once I would have liked the joy of being the one to surprise Mutti with some bread.

In just a few minutes we reached our home. When all our safety checks were made and we felt nobody was watching us, we opened the huge, heavy door, dashed up the steps, and slipped into our little apartment. Mutti and Onkel Emil couldn't believe their eyes. A whole loaf of bread? Dieter, with his face aglow, proudly told the fairy tale he had just experienced. A trip on a motorcycle and bread? That was almost too much for anyone to believe.

When we were all set for our devotions, Mutti was heartbroken to realize that her Bible had remained behind on the table at Onkel Lehmann's house. Onkel Emil had not had his Bible for some time. It was lost with his luggage on the trip to Lippehne.

"We will now have to search our hearts and see how much Scripture we have memorized." Mutti opened our spiritual time.

"Let's see, children, how much of God's Word we have hidden in our hearts. But first we'll start with a song. Let's sing."

Because I am Jesus's little sheep
I am glad for evermore
My good shepherd knows me and cares for me
He loves me and calls me by my name.

"Yes, Mutti," Marlies said excitedly, "He loves me, too." Her curls bounced around her head when she moved and talked. She was so cute. "I like to sing that song all the time," she continued. Suddenly she began to sing a solo of "Jesus Loves Me." When our little soloist was finished, we all sang in whispering tones "God is Love, He Came to Redeem Me" and many other beautiful songs. Onkel Emil started quoting scripture. When my turn came I quoted John 3:16: "For God so loved the world, that he gave his only begotten Son, that whosoever believeth in him should not perish, but have everlasting life."

"Does that mean He loves the Russians, too, Mutti?" My brother looked puzzled.

"Of course Jesus does, Dieter. God sent His Son for the whole world, for every human being. You see, the Lord does not care whether you are Russian or German. Neither does He care if you are rich or poor. He is concerned, however, whether you are going to heaven or hell. He is concerned about each one making the right decision. He wants everybody to be forgiven of his sins and to live in heaven with Him."

"I see."

"Now here are my verses," Mutti said. "He that dwelleth in the secret place of the most High shall abide under the shadow of the Almighty. I will say of the Lord, He is my refuge and my fortress: my God; in him will I trust."

Then Onkel Emil joined Mutti, "Surely he shall deliver thee from the snare of the fowler, and from the noisome pestilence." Alone he continued, "Thou shalt not be afraid for the terror by night; nor for the arrow that flieth by day."

"How comforting," Mutti added.

"Let's all pray now," Onkel Emil continued. "We thank You, Lord, for using our enemies to sustain us. We belong to You, Lord, and we thank You that we can always depend on You to sustain us.

"You know the whereabouts of our loved ones. Please keep my wife safe and strong. Watch over my daughters. Keep Emmy's husband and the father of these children from harm. We pray for Kaetchen and all the others upstairs, even those we don't know; please keep them safe."

"Forgive us where we have displeased You and sinned against You. Cover all of our sins with Your blood. It is too difficult for me to understand why You, the Almighty, even show concern for us and love us, but we thank You for everything. I pray this in Jesus's name. Amen."

During the night, the passageway was filled with noisy and drunken soldiers. We heard them stomping up the longer wooden stairs which led to the apartments of the sisters and several other young ladies. The next morning silence had set in again, and we noticed that the huge passage door was wide open, completely covering our small door.

In the following days our begging trips often yielded nothing edible, but we were usually successful in finding firewood. Mutti was busy all day caring for Marlies and Udo. Both of them were crying more every day because of hunger, and Mutti's biggest problem was keeping them quiet. I felt so sad every time I saw her cupping her hand over Udo's mouth so his crying couldn't be heard. There was nothing to eat besides a few potatoes that Dieter and I had found at the cache several days ago.

The next morning Onkel Emil could no longer endure the little ones' suffering, and he decided to risk his life by going out in search of food or a job.

"Surely the Russians will not harm a one-legged old invalid of World War I," he whispered jokingly as he prepared to leave.

"We can't predict what they may or may not do, Emil. So please, be careful," Mutti advised.

We all helped check the street and passage before we gave Onkel Emil the signal that it was safe to step outside. He didn't return until late in the afternoon, but his face was aglow. Onkel Emil handed Mutti a can, that contained about one pint of watery soup, and one slice of dark bread. "This is my wage for the day," he announced proudly. "I am the tailor for the Russian commander, and he wanted me to find other Germans who are capable of doing tailoring and organize a tailor shop. We are to sew uniforms for the Russians. The pay will be one can of soup and one slice of bread per day."

"This is cabbage soup. Thank you, Emil!" Mutti said in a voice filled with emotion. "You are a wonderful help to me and my children. Congratulations on your new job, too. You'll have to tell me later how you expect to go about setting up your tailor shop and how you plan to find your personnel. But right now I'll heat up the soup and feed my starving children."

Each day from then on we gave thanks for the soup Onkel Emil brought home for us. He needed nourishment, too, but was kind and selfless. Even though his ration put some food into our stomachs, we still continued to suffer from hunger pangs.

One day, after returning from work, Onkel Emil paid Kaetchen and the others a visit. He learned that they were barely surviving on the few supplies the sisters still had and Onkel Lehmann's wage for the work he continued to do for the Russians, one slice of bread per day. Every night the noisy and drunken Russians visited the two young women in the next apartment, but none of the others had been molested. Onkel Emil called our attention to the fact that we had already been away from the farm for two months.

"It is a miracle, a real miracle," he said, "that we have lived in complete safety throughout all that time. During the hours of greatest danger, the night hours when the open season on women begins, the Lord always keeps us hidden behind the passage door."

Dieter and I continued our hunts for food, day after long, cold day. Often we found things for which we were not looking. "Why are they taking the skin off the man's head, Liane?" Dieter asked nonchalantly as we walked past the window of a home.

"What are you saying? Taking off skin?"

"Yes, look in that window."

We doubled back, and I was truly scared when I saw the gruesome sight. Dieter was right. An autopsy was being performed right in front of the low window of a home. The sight of it made me shiver. Both of us suddenly found ourselves running along the streets of Lippehne. We were running without knowing why, and we arrived at home totally out of breath, with just a few pieces of firewood under our arms. I think we forgot to return to the lake for more wood.

Another day we found a much more pleasant surprise. "Close your eyes and open your hands, Mutti," we whispered after our return home.

Mutti squeezed her eyes shut and stretched both hands out in front of her.

"Pussy willows and a birch branch?" Mutti said totally surprised. "Is it spring?" She began to weep.

"We don't want you to cry, Mutti. We want you to be happy."

"It is spring, and I didn't even know it here in our little ark. You children are like the dove that told Noah that the waters had receded and that there was life outside the ark." Then she hugged us. "Thank you, children! Thank you, Lord, for showing Your love to me! Thank you for showing me that Your love is as fresh as spring every day!"

In the midst of our excitement, a timid tap on our door told us that a friend must be visiting us. How thrilled we were to see Onkel Lehmann. He had decided, at great risk, to return to the farm to check on things there, and he had come to tell us about his experiences.

"I knocked on the door and was amazed that the officer invited me in. I informed him that I just wanted to get a few things and look around. He was very friendly and gave me permission to do so. I noticed immediately that several pieces of furniture were missing and decided to go upstairs to check on the two sewing machines. What I saw there proved to me again that we have a God who cares about His children. You remember, Emmy, that the two machines were standing in the attic side by side: your new cabinet-type Singer machine and my wife's old treadle machine. Well, my wife's machine is gone, but, believe it or not, yours is still standing in the same spot."

"You mean they took the old machine and left my new one? The Lord must have struck them with blindness! Maybe they didn't consider the small table to be a machine. I have had the feeling for some time that it will be my sewing that will keep my children alive, and now I know that for certain. Thank you, Onkel Lehmann, for the wonderful news! I just have to pray now that the machine will remain there until we return to your little farm. Did they say anything about when we'll be able to return?"

"I asked them, but they didn't answer me."

A few days later, just as Dieter and I were in the process of dragging firewood into the passage, we noticed that Kaetchen was knocking gently on our door.

"Emmy," she said excitedly when Mutti opened the door. But the smile quickly vanished from her face when she saw Mutti reaching for Udo's mouth and holding it shut. "Emmychen, I am sorry—how long can our children endure this?"

"He is crying all the time now. I can't let him cry out loud. We can't let them find us here."

"Our poor children. How sad I feel. Here is a little piece of bread for you and a little flour."

"Thank you, Kaetchen, thank you so much! Where did you get this?"

"I went to our little farm. Since the officers there were kind enough to my dad, I decided to walk home myself and ask for some food. One of them inquired as to what we need. I told him that we have nothing to eat and would really appreciate some fat, a little sugar, and some potatoes. He said he would place food for me in the courtyard under the old cover of my mother's first sewing machine, so that no one else would see it. It seems they have to be very careful even among themselves. After looking around a little, I went outside and was surprised that the officer had indeed kept his promise. He really had placed some food under the cover. It was another miracle. Without our Lord caring for us so miraculously, we definitely would not have survived this long. So take these few things, Emmy, and feed your starving son."

The two mothers encouraged each other for a few moments before Kaetchen quietly slipped back upstairs.

Kaetchen's visit had refreshed Mutti, and she even sang while Udo and Marlies were munching on a piece of bread.

Mutti began preparing our dinner. "We will have klunker-suppe tonight," she told us joyfully.

"Klunkersuppe? We haven't had that in half a year."

"Yes, I think you are right. It has been a long time. Why don't you cook it for us tonight, Schaefle?"

"I hope I still remember how to prepare it." I thought hard. "Let me see. You bring the water to a boiling point, add a pinch of cattle salt, and then drop the little moistened lumps of flour into the boiling water, right? Then you let it boil for a few minutes and what do you have? The most wonderful soup ever for our empty stomachs."

"Perfect, Schaefle. Just perfect."

That night, even though I had been busy all day, it was very difficult for me to fall asleep. The ruckus from the drunken soldiers in the passageway was louder than ever. Suddenly screams pierced through the courtyard.

"Help! Help! Lord, help me!" Voices of young women rent the air, and men's voices answered with cruel laughter. I buried my head in the feather bed, hoping for silence, but the drunken brawling continued to be mingled with the screams of women. Was there no one to help them? The cries of pain and agony absolutely horrified me. How I wished there was something I could do. There I was, safe in bed; what was happening to them? I tried to envision things, and wondered if Kaetchen was one of them. Heavy boots constantly stomped upstairs to the apartments. Throughout the night screams of girls and women filtered into our little home.

"God, why are You so good to us?" I asked. "So many are suffering right now and we are safe here in Your ark. Why, Lord? Why?" There was really no way for me to answer my own questions, except that I thought God must have a special purpose for keeping us alive and safe. If so, I reasoned, then nothing would be able to harm us until the Lord allowed it. With that comforting thought, I was finally able to get some sleep.

When I awakened in the morning, the sun was shining brightly. Everything was quiet and peaceful, and I was certain that the horrible screams of the previous night were probably just a bad dream. Before I was able to set my thoughts in order, Kaetchen walked into our room. Was I relieved to see her that day!

"Praise the Lord for protecting us all through another night, Emmychen!" she said, bubbling with excitement. "We were safe again under the shadow of the Almighty. Did I mention to you before how we always bolt our door and secure it with a heavy log? Well, last night someone was beating on the door during all that screaming, and before we could open it, a Russian, a messenger of God, broke through the door."

"What did you say? A Russian a messenger of God?"

"Yes, Emmy! My dad was on his knees, crying before the Lord and interceding for all of those whose screams we heard.

The Russian recognized my dad as one who had worked for him and said, motioning at all the frightened ladies in our room: 'You are father here? No afraid. Me back.' And with those remarks he left. A short time later he returned with bacon and bread. Can you imagine that? Bacon and bread?"

Mutti was speechless.

"We have a gracious God, Emmy, don't we? You or I could have been one of those who were tortured and raped last night by those drunken beasts." Both women embraced and wept uncontrollably.

Several days later, in early May, the streets were filled with jubilant Russians. "Hitler kaputt!" they hollered. "Hitler kaputt!" What did this mean? Could this mean the war had ended? Everyone was guessing, but no one seemed to have an answer. On his way home from work Onkel Emil heard the same expressions of joy from Russians in the streets: "Hitler kaputt! Hitler kaputt!" Onkel Emil also shared another story he heard at work. His coworkers told him of a line-up of Germans who were to be shot because one of the Russian comrades was found dead.

"You Germans kill comrade. You kill friend," Russians yelled to those in the line-up. In order to prove the Germans guilty, an autopsy was performed publicly in the town square. To the embarrassment of all those watching, the autopsy showed that the soldier died of nothing other than an overconsumption of alcohol. Instead of being shot, the frightened Germans were set free.

All through the night drunken Russians celebrated by yelling, hollering, and shooting in the streets. "Hitler kaputt! Germany kaputt!" These phrases filtered into our little home continuously, along with screams and sobs from women and girls. Bottles or dishes were smashed against the passage walls, and none of us was able to sleep.

"What will happen if the war is really over?" Mutti asked Onkel Emil the next morning. "What will we do? Will we stay here? Where else can we go? How can we find our loved ones?"

These questions and many more went back and forth like ping-pong balls.

"How can we make any plans if we don't know for certain that the war has ended?" Onkel Emil said. "Perhaps these are just rumors. I can't believe that the Germans gave up so easily. Hitler

67

would fight, fight, fight for us. How can you even consider that the war is over, Emmy?"

"Do you really believe, Emil, that God would not punish Germany for the way Hitler moved with destruction into foreign lands and uprooted people? Even more, Hitler degraded God's chosen people by taking away their businesses and burning their synagogues. Had they harmed anybody? No! They lived peacefully among us. Then he decided to mark every Jewish person by having him wear the yellow Star of David on his clothing. Look how much we have suffered—and we were supposedly Hitler's people. That same man hated Jews. So we probably have no idea how much more they have suffered! I believe, as I think you do, too, that any crime committed against God's people is a crime committed against God. Do you think God can quietly overlook all of this? He wouldn't be a righteous God if He did."

"Yes, I agree. But the problem is that those who did not support Hitler now also have to suffer. Look at the predicament in which we find ourselves. Our families are ripped apart. We are barely surviving. All of this because of one man who set out to conquer the world. If we couldn't cling to our Father right now, things would be utterly hopeless for us. What would we do without our faith and without the anticipation of our heavenly home? How could we even exist without the knowledge that He is still in control of the universe?"

"I don't know," Mutti replied sadly as she turned to Udo and Marlies who were crying bitterly, but softly. "I really don't know. I just don't see how you can still believe in Hitler and his miracle weapons and his miracle powers. Hasn't that man put us through enough yet? Are you by any chance a Nazi yourself?"

"What do you think, Emmy? Can a born-again Christian be a Nazi?" Onkel Emil seemed insulted that she had asked such a question.

At mid-morning, Onkel Lehmann came to our door with the exciting news that the Russians had vacated his little farm.

"Let's all return home as quickly as possible," he suggested, "before anyone else moves into the house."

Hurriedly Mutti and I packed our few belongings and put coats on the little ones. Dieter and I brought the handwagon from the courtyard and began placing our bundles in it. Kaetchen, Onkel Lehmann, and his two grandsons were just scrambling down the stairs. They added their bundles to the wagon. With Udo perched in the middle of everything, we took off over the bumpy, centuries-old cobblestones. We encountered no soldiers on the streets as our small parade moved to the end of the block and turned left toward the little farm. Dieter and his friend, Hanno, were happy to see each other after so many weeks.

"This warm spring air is so refreshing, Emmychen, isn't it?" Kaetchen bubbled.

"Oh, yes! I think Noah and his family must have felt this way when they left the ark."

"Will you tell us that story tonight, Mutti?" Dieter pleaded. "You tell the story, and when you come to the animals I'll name them."

"We'll do that, my son."

"Bow-wow, bow-wow!" Udo tried to bark when he heard the word "animals."

7
Home Again

The green front door of our little farmhouse was wide open when we arrived, and the boys were so excited about being home again that they could hardly be restrained. Eagerly they tried to run into the house, but Onkel Lehmann held them back.

"I'll go in first and check things out. I don't want you fellows to encounter danger. You may come as far as the hallway and wait there."

"The house stinks," Hanno said to those of us still standing outside as he held his nose. "It stinks terribly."

"Horribly terribly!" Dieter chimed in. "Phew! Phew!"

"I guess it is safe," Onkel Lehmann reported. "I can't see anyone anywhere."

We started bringing the bundles into our home, and soon everyone was in agreement that the house stank terribly. Mutti carried bundles upstairs, and I followed her with Udo. Suddenly I heard her cough and gag. When I reached her, I realized that she was vomiting.

"What is the matter, Mutti?" I asked, but found the answer myself. The laundry tub, right next to our room, was filled to overflowing with human waste. Kaetchen rushed upstairs to check on all the commotion, and when she saw the tub, she also got sick.

Mutti had left a note for Onkel Emil, so before too long he arrived at the farmhouse, knocking on the door in Morse code. Onkel Lehmann let him in, but Onkel Emil's joy was short-lived as well when he smelled and saw what Russian culture had done to our home.

"How will we ever get rid of this mess?" he wondered aloud. "I believe Onkel Lehmann and I will have to be in charge of emptying the kettle, since the stomachs of both of you women are so weak. We'll have to carry the waste to a field bucket by bucket."

"Have you seen the outhouse yet, Emil?" Mutti asked.

"No, I haven't."

That, too, looked beyond description. Feces were piled high all around the seat, in the corners, and on the floor.

When darkness set in, Mutti and I had accomplished quite a bit in setting our room in order.

"We'll have to clean the rest of it tomorrow," Mutti told me. "We accomplished quite a bit today in cleaning and discarding filthy rags. What I can't understand, though, is that after all that work, the house still stinks. We'll probably have to clean for weeks to get this place back in order."

What a joyful time of devotions we had that night. We were reunited again, and we were all back home.

"Thank you, Lord," Onkel Lehmann prayed, "for being so good to us. You are the great Creator, and You have shown us over and over that You do not forsake those who trust in You. You have kept us safe while we were apart, and You graciously returned our home to us. Lord, we thank You. Every day You become more precious to us. Earthly possessions mean less now than they did a few short months ago. Lord, may we not cling to anything or desire anything but You.

"Lord, I pray for our enemies. Let us somehow be a blessing to them. Let them see that we love You. O Lord, don't forget all the people of this town, those who are still at home, and those who are on a journey somewhere. Please don't let our neighbors forget the promises they made to You in this very room. Forgive us where we have sinned today. O Lord, place all of our shortcomings under Your blood. Lord, we love You and we praise You and we thank You. In the name of Your precious Son, Jesus. Amen."

When we awakened the next morning, our room still stank.

"I'll help you clean for a while, Mutti, before Dieter and I go begging. I'll scrub the floor for you."

"That's good, Schaefle, thank you. I'll scrub some more of the filth in the attic while you finish this room."

With a hand broom and dust pan I started sweeping under the bed and became excited.

"Mutti, come see what I found. Why didn't we look under the bed sooner? Our curtains are back there."

Stretching out on the floor on my stomach, I slid under the bed, reached for the curtains, and slid back out.

"How disgusting! Mutti, come and see. The curtains have been torn into pieces and guess what's wrapped inside?"

"Sick! Sick! Sick!" Mutti said, and her whole body seemed to go into convulsions. "That is Russian culture! Dung wrapped in curtains!"

With the broom I shoved the lace curtains onto the dustpan and dumped them into the garbage. Mutti helped me move the heavy bed, and I continued scrubbing the floor. Suddenly I heard Mutti making strange noises in the attic. "What is the matter, Mutti?" I called, rushing to her. She just stood there, with her right hand pointing at her discovery: our canning jars, lined up near the sewing machine, were filled with human waste.

After days of vomiting, gagging, scrubbing, and discarding, Mutti and Kaetchen finally turned our sickening situation around.

Onkel Emil enjoyed his work at the tailor shop and was thrilled to hand Mutti his soup and piece of bread every night. Along with other Germans whom he had recruited and trained, he was a valuable tailor for the Russians. Onkel Lehmann had been recruited by the Russians from his digging work to guard the pianos and sewing machines that they had taken out of homes. The valuable items stood at the railroad station for months, covered with snow or soaked from rain. Not one piece had been shipped to Russia because of the destruction of the railroad tracks.

Shocking and disgusting were the ways of many of the Russian guards at the school across the street. Dieter and I eventually had to quit taking our shortcut by way of the promenades because of one character who stood, always against the same tree at the entrance, making obscene gestures and keeping his privy part exposed. The searching of homes and raping of women continued as new troops regularly moved into Lippehne.

Since the war had ended, we were able to have more contact with other Germans. Being less isolated, however, also brought more sorrows. We learned of all kinds of atrocities that had ruined the lives of Germans in various ways. The mind of a neighbor's beautiful fifteen-year-old daughter snapped one day after continual public rapings by the Russians. She acted and talked like a baby.

The twenty-five-year-old mayor's daughter was forced to help clear the town of rubbish and cadavers. As guards stood over her with their rifles, her spade hit a body. It was that of her father. He had been missing for several months. Two of Onkel Lehmann's young female church members were suffering great physical pain because of the many rapings they had had to endure. The wounded hands of those whose fingers had been chopped off by the Russians, so they could take the gold wedding bands, were healing very poorly without medical attention.

One day another order reached the few Germans left in Lippehne. From the Russian Commander it came: all Germans must leave. Only those considered valuable to the Russian labor force—Onkel Emil, the tailor, and Mutti, who assisted him by working at home—were to stay. Since we lived with Onkel Lehmann and Kaetchen, they were also allowed to stay. Some of the Germans rounded up two weak and undernourished horses to pull a hay wagon laden with sick and old people. For us, the worst meaning of the order was that Omi and my aunt would have to go also, since they were no longer living in Onkel Lehmann's house.

"Mutti, I don't want them to leave! Omi can't leave us!" Even to myself, I was beginning to sound frantic.

"Oh, Schaefle, how I wish we could do something to keep her and my sister-in-law with us longer, but we can't. Only the Lord can comfort us now. Only the Lord knows if we will ever see them again."

"God be with you till we meet again," Mutti said with tears streaming down her face as she kissed her mother-in-law. Silently weeping, she gave her sister-in-law a hug. I just wanted to hold on to Omi and not let her go. Her face was so etched in sorrow that I could hardly bear to look at her. We only embraced and cried. Our sweet Omi, Vati's wonderful mother. Why did she have to leave us? And my aunt, why? Why? I didn't think I would ever get over it; not as long as I lived. Omi sat on the wagon while my aunt followed on foot. Brokenhearted we stood and watched our loved ones slowly turn the next street corner. War! War! I hate it, I thought. It kills! It separates!

After that, the languages Dieter and I heard on our begging trips were no longer German and Russian, but Polish and Russian. The Polish people were being brought to Lippehne by the Russians to help them claim the conquered land. The Poles were very angry people because the communists had forced them out of their homes. In Lippehne they were given the privilege to move into any home they chose. Those arriving first continued, as had the conquerors, to loot and steal from the few Germans who were still in town. They rushed from one vacated house to another, helping themselves to whatever they needed and wanted. They burglarized and harassed the Germans, after the 9:00 P.M. curfew especially. They, and everyone else, were aware of the fact that to go and report a crime during the curfew hours called for immediate arrest. This law made the Germans and their belongings an open prey for anyone.

One day while searching through a farm for something edible, my brother and I climbed into the attic and found a pile of small seeds.

"Wheat! Wheat! We have found wheat!" Dieter called excitedly.

"No, that is not wheat, and it isn't rye either. I remember what grain looks like. Opi had fields of it on his farm. But this is not wheat. Don't you remember how we used to play hide and seek among the sheaves in the field? We used to call the eight or ten sheaves, which were leaning against one another to dry, our houses; and we always sat inside, munching on kernels of wheat or rye. Those kernels didn't look like these."

"I remember the playing part, but I don't remember what the seeds looked like. I also remember the storks always walking between our houses and gobbling up the frogs. Do you remember the racket they made when they stood on their huge wagon wheel nest and clapped their beaks? Every morning when I wanted to sleep, they woke me up with their beaks."

"Did Opi ever tell you, Dieter, that the same stork couple had come back to the same nest every spring for fifteen years?"

"They must have liked that huge wheel Opi put in the tree for them to build their nest on. But how did we get on the stork subject?"

"It all started with the seeds."

"Anyway, I don't know what kind of seeds these are. Let's take some home and see if Mutti can use them. I think I saw a small bucket downstairs. We can scoop them into that, and if they are edible we'll come back for more."

"You children," Mutti greeted us. "You scavengers—where did you find millet?"

"In the attic, on a farm," Dieter answered proudly. "We can get more. Would you like more?"

"What can you do with millet?" I still wasn't sure about those strange-looking seeds.

"We can grind it and make flour. We'll grind it in the coffee grinder, a little bit at a time."

Kaetchen came and joined the excited group. "It will take us a long time to turn this into flour, but with everybody helping we will be done in no time."

"And think of the nutritious millet soup and millet pancakes we'll enjoy," Mutti added.

Dieter, the little provider, seemed so proud to help. "Let's go, Liane, and get the rest of the millet seeds."

Later that day, after the rest of the millet had been safely cached, Mutti gathered us four together. "Today, children," Mutti announced, "I want to hear you recite your poems. We haven't done that in several days, and we must make sure that we are ready for Vati's homecoming. You start, my little son. Can you say your lines?"

Udo stood up straight and tall, hands at his sides and intermingled with some baby talk said,

Vati, dear Vati, I greet you today.
I pray that you never again go away.

When he had finished, he dashed into Mutti's arms for his reward, a hug.

Then Marlies, the little charmer, placed herself in front of us and curtsied:

Vati, O Vati, I love you today.
Will you stay home so that we can play?
I waited so-o-o-o long to see your face
And know that it is only God's grace
That we can all be together again
And with you love Jesus and not be afraid.
I am so glad you are at our house.
I love you, Vati. Your little Pittimaus.

Another quick curtsy and with two leaps she was in Mutti's lap. Dieter's and my poems were considerably longer, and Mutti took in every word. Our performance seemed to please her because her face was glowing with pride and joy. "Vati will be so proud of you and so happy to see you all. We must pray more that our reunion will be soon."

"We must pray for Hanno and Vilmar's Vati, too," Marlies added. "Vilmar cried yesterday. He misses his Vati," she recounted with a sad face.

"Yes, we will pray for him, too."

As we sat on the couch in our room we all prayed for a long time for everyone we knew, especially for Omi, my aunt, and Vati. We had no idea where any of them might be, or what they might be suffering.

Our water situation was becoming serious. We had learned to live with only two hours of running city water daily. For the past few days, however, we had had no water at all. Hauling water from a large well in the town square had become another new assignment for Dieter and me. We pumped our buckets only half full so that they were not too heavy for us to carry home. For several days we helped supply water for our needs. When the city again returned to the two hours of running water, we filled every pot, tub, and bottle in the house, just in case the supply would be turned off again. During bath time that week, we would really have to conserve.

"There is no other way but for all of us to use the same bath water," Kaetchen announced after dinner. "Of course we can't use much soap either since our supply is almost exhausted. Lathering will not be allowed. A few hand turns around the soap per person is it. I suggest, Emmychen, we go by age. What do you think?"

"That is a splendid idea."

"I don't plan to participate in the 'bathathon,' " Onkel Lehmann said. "I must disagree with the concept that it is a splendid idea. You'll have one less, then."

"Well, we start with Udo. He is the only one who gets clean water," Mutti told everyone and started to get him ready. The scum was scooped off the top of the water after each person. I was glad I was number six in line and not the last one like Onkel Emil. No one complained, though, and everyone was thankful for the bath and for being able to greet the Lord's day with a clean feeling.

"God, Creator of the universe," Onkel Lehmann prayed during our Sunday service, "we praise You for Your goodness to us. We thank You for Your love to us, for sending Your only Son for us, and for the uncounted blessings You have given us.

"Thank You for Your daily protection and the miracle of sustaining us on so little food. Lord, You know our bodies continue to weaken, and some of us struggle with boils. Heal us if it is Your will.

"We commit all of our loved ones to You and our neighbors who have had to leave, wherever they are today, and our enemies."

As Onkel Lehmann's voice went on, I realized the prayer must have been too long for Udo. He had fallen asleep.

One day at the old bakery, Dieter and I noticed people standing in line. The smell of fresh bread filled the street and made us hungry. We walked to the end of the line and stood there along with everyone else, waiting to get into the store. When I took a closer look at the Polish ladies, I realized that they all looked rather sad. All of them were wearing scarves to cover their hair, and few of them talked. They just stared and appeared oblivious to everything going on around them. When, after about an hour and a half of waiting, we stepped up to the counter to ask for bread, we were told that we could not buy bread without Polish money. Polish money? Where could we get Polish zlotys? Dieter broke down and cried. "Where can we get zlotys?"

A few days later, a Polish lady came to our house carrying a bag of fur pieces. She had heard about Mutti's sewing ability and asked her to sew a fur coat. She would pay Mutti in zlotys when the coat was finished. For a whole week Mutti worked every day and by candlelight throughout the greater part of the night. The promise of getting Polish currency for her sewing gave Mutti the added energy to finish the sewing project. How delighted she was when her customer gave her five hundred zlotys for the work.

"I'll go to town today," she said joyfully, "to the new grocery store. I wonder what I can buy with all this money. What our bodies need most right now is fat. That is one item I definitely plan to purchase." She disguised herself as an old grandmother. She put on a long, black dress, covered her beautiful curls with a black scarf, and hobbled up the street with a cane.

When Mutti returned, Kaetchen opened the door to let her in. Mutti scuffed into the hallway, pushing one foot in front of the other, back bent low, breathing heavily.

"Emmychen, you look very uninviting," Kaetchen jested. "Is that how you moved through town?"

"You better believe it!"

The two friends laughed so hard that they had to hold their stomachs.

"Now let me see you move to the end of the hallway again, Great-grandmother! You are a wonderful actress! How I wish I had a camera to take a picture of you," Kaetchen giggled. "Tell me now, what did you purchase with all that money? I've been so caught up in the drama and excitement of your acting, I almost forgot to ask what you were able to buy with your riches."

"Well, Kaetchen, here it is. My week's wage yielded one pound of butter and nothing else."

"That is all you got for five hundred zlotys?"

"That is all."

"Is the butter fresh?"

"Funny, Kaetchen, you should ask that. I never thought of checking. I was just so happy to get it." As Mutti and Kaetchen unwrapped the butter, they didn't even have to hold it close to their noses. The butter was rancid.

However great our disappointment, the news that Mutti was an excellent seamstress quickly spread through the Polish community. Several women brought their fabrics and ordered dresses. Mutti no longer accepted money as payment, but requested food. Dieter and I were also becoming more deeply involved in Mutti's new sewing business. We took our buckets and walked to the other side of the lake to the homes that had been destroyed on the night of the invasion of Lippehne. There we searched through the ruins for charcoal, which Mutti used in her flatiron. As Mutti's business increased, our trips to the ruins also became more frequent. Occasionally we found Russian soldiers and asked them for bread. Our Russian vocabulary continued to grow, and we were now able to approach them in their own language. The smell of garlic on their breath seemed stronger during these summer days and their uniforms now consisted of olive-green pants, blouse-like shirts, and leather belts. Without their hats they seemed funny to us because they were all shorn. "No lice that way," one of them told us when Dieter asked.

Late in the spring, a day of celebration came to us. One of Mutti's customers, a farmer's wife, came to pick up her dress and insisted that Dieter and I return to her farm with her. We couldn't understand why, but Mutti trusted her and let us go. It was a warm, sunny day. Walking through town, we followed the lady across one open field after another. It seemed we would never get to the farm, but finally she pointed it out to us in the distance. She tried to converse with us in Polish, but we didn't understand one word. Upon arriving at the farm, the heavy-set lady took us to her kitchen and offered us each a cup of milk.

"Danke schoen, danke schoen," Dieter said as he reached for his and quickly gulped it down. How I wished I could talk to the kind lady! I would have told her that we hadn't had a drop of milk since January, and how much we appreciated her kindness.

She was dipping into her huge can again, filling a small aluminum can with milk. She handed it to me. To Dieter she gave a loaf of bread and a piece of lard wrapped in paper.

"Go home!" she said with a big grin which pulled up her rosy cheeks to look like small balloons. "Go home!" After we thanked her again, she opened the door for us, and we left.

"Do you think Udo will like the milk?" Dieter asked excitedly.

"He will, even though he doesn't know what it is. He is too small to remember milk."

"I don't think he is small. He will be two years old soon."

"That is true, but he can't remember things yet as well as you and I can."

On our way home we tried to imagine what Mutti and Kaetchen would say when they saw our treasures.

"Let's sit down here for a while, Dieter, in the soft, green grass and take a rest."

A lark, Mutti's favorite bird, was singing beautifully as I watched the clouds which hardly seemed to move. In a hedgerow nearby, I saw a sparrow preening itself. How peaceful it was here in the country. There seemed to be nothing to fear.

As we were sitting, watching the birds fly by, Dieter finally could contain himself no longer, "Do you think I could have some of that milk? I could use the lid for a cup. Then it won't be so heavy for you to carry, either."

"No, Dieter. Absolutely not. We are going to carry every drop in this can home. I'm sure, though, that Mutti will give you a little more when we get back."

Both of us fought down the temptation to lighten our load by eating some of our wonderful gifts, but we did not yield and arrived home with every drop of milk and every crumb of bread.

"You brought milk and bread and lard? This is just unbelievable. A miracle!" Mutti rejoiced when we showed her.

"Praise the Lord! We can't believe it!" and more expressions of this kind sprang forth from both Mutti and Kaetchen. What a feast we would have! But why was Mutti crying? Could it have been that she was so happy because her undernourished children would drink milk that day?

1. Emil and Emmy (Krueger) Guddat on their wedding day, December 26, 1932.

2. The Krueger family, 1925. (L-R) Emmy, Johanna, Erich, August, and Gertrud.

3. Ludwig Borrmann, great-grandfather, in 1944. He was shot by the Russians at age 93.

3

2

4. *"Opi" Guddat with Dieter and Liane, 1939.*

5. *Emil's family: Gustav and Henriette Guddat with Fritz and Martha, 1939.*

6. *An old handwagon. Some people still use them today.*

5

4

6

7. *The Guddats in 1943.*
Emil Guddat was a
supply officer in the
German army. Here he is
shown with Emmy,
Dieter, Liane, and
Marlies. Udo was not yet
born.

7

8

8. *The Reverend Ernst*
Lehmann, November
1944.

9. The building where Liane and Dieter went to school, looking virtually the same as it did in 1944.

10

11

12

13

*10. Kaetchen
Mecklenburg with Hanno
and Vilmar in 1944.*

*11. Kaetchen, after
severe stress and near
starvation, with her sons
less than two years later.*

*12. The hospital where
Onkel Lehmann died.*

13. The lake in Lippehne.

14. A train is overrun with refugees who were desperate for any means of transportation.

15. A post-war scene from the once-glamorous city of Berlin: what was left of the Brandenburg Gate in 1945.

15

16. The house that once belonged to Onkel Lehmann, as it was in 1976. Very little has been altered, and the window from which Emmy climbed to the chimney is still in the roof.

16

17. *The Guddats in the refugee camp, Nienburg/Weser, West Germany, Christmas, 1949.*

18. *The crowded life of a refugee camp. People lived in such conditions for months and years at a time.*

19. Emil Schmidtke and wife, Amalie, in 1952.

20. The Guddat family in 1982. On their golden wedding anniversary, Emil and Emmy are shown with their children (L-R) Marlies (Blaskowski), Dieter, Udo, and Liane (Brown).

21. Emil and Emmy Guddat with Wilhelm and Kaetchen Mecklenburg, Easter, 1981, in Boca Raton, Florida.

8
Times of Testing

A new influx of Russian soldiers made our lives become more restless and fearful again. One night all of us were huddled in one room when, at about 10:00 P.M., someone beat furiously on the front door. Onkel Emil limped to the door, but before he could open it completely, the impatient soldiers forced it open, ramming him into the hallway wall. They raced from room to room, aiming their flashlights at the faces of the sleeping children, under the beds, and anywhere they thought a German soldier, or a woman, might hide. After an unsuccessful hunt, they looked in vain for vodka and food. The farm yard, coal shed, and barn didn't yield anything either.

"German woman beautiful," one of the soldiers said as he ripped Mutti's black scarf from her head. "Not this. Why this?"

"Because German woman afraid. Afraid of Ruski," Mutti answered.

"Not be afraid, woman. Ruski wants love German woman." With that he tried to embrace her, but she pushed him away. His persistence made her angry, and she continued to fight to free herself. Suddenly, the soldier realized that his comrades had left, and he dashed out of the room. Most nights brought incidents such as that. It was very unusual to have a calm night, especially since there were Polish troops now, also, who searched houses and stole whatever they desired.

Daytime had its own surprises. One morning a Polish soldier banged on the door. "Woman, come," he commanded when Kaetchen answered. "Come work."

"You have to wait," she said boldly. "I have to dress my children first. I have to take them along." With that, she left him standing in the hallway and went to dress Hanno and Vilmar, who were still in their pajamas.

When she returned with her sons, the impatient soldier yanked her by the arm and repeated, "Woman, come!"

"I'm coming. I'm coming."

Mutti leaned over the bannister and whispered, "We'll pray, Kaetchen. Goodbye!"

"Lord, please protect them," Mutti pleaded as we all gathered around her. "Watch over them and let no evil befall them. I also place Dieter and Liane in Your care again as they go begging. You have been so good to us. Show Yourself to all of us today in a mighty way. Blessed be Your name. Amen."

I usually tried to catch up on my darning before we left to go begging, since those projects took up most of my spare time. As sock fibers weakened, everyone's holes continually became larger. There was no time left for my favorite pastime, knitting. The only socks I didn't have to darn were the woolen knee socks I had knitted for Dieter. They were still in perfect condition in spite of the fact that they had to be washed so often. His bandages sometimes slipped, and the boils would seep right into his socks.

"Why do you think the Russian is watching us, Liane?" Dieter asked later as we walked along the mirror-like lake in search of firewood.

"I didn't realize somebody was watching us."

My eyes moved toward the gardens along the promenade. I saw the Russian with a rifle slung across his back, beginning to move in our direction. He approached us with a big smile on his face and told us that he wanted to learn German. He pointed at trees, flowers, houses, and gates, and wanted to know the German word for each one of them. Then he began pointing at different articles of clothing I wore, and I continued to give him the German equivalent.

Dieter was becoming rather bored with the lessons. He raced to the water's edge to perfect his skill at skipping pebbles across the lake. As the learning session went on, the Russian touched me and wanted to know the word for underwear. My heart had been racing from the moment he began talking to us, but now it threatened to jump out of my chest. It pounded and pounded, loud and hard. I pushed back his hand.

You must get away, my mind told me. I took one step back and the Russian took one forward. Would he shoot me if I ran? I could see his smiling face turning angry.

Take a chance. Run! Run! Run! something told me. Scarcely realizing what I was doing, I whirled around and dashed away. I heard a rifle being cocked behind me. Heavy footsteps followed. I just knew this was life's end, but I still ran. I waited for a shot to ring out. *Do it fast, please!* I thought. The rifle cocked again. I couldn't try to duck or dodge the bullet—he would catch up to me then. *Run! Run! Faster!* My mind screamed at me, but I was moving as fast as I possibly could. I couldn't run faster.

As I dashed across the school yard, I realized that the sound of stomping boots was growing fainter. *Run! Run! Just a few more seconds!* I could see our house across the street. Never before had it been such a welcome sight. Totally out of breath, I stopped just short of the front door. "Thank you, Lord, for fast-moving legs." I gasped half-aloud. Glancing back for the first time, I saw no Russian anywhere. But was he watching from somewhere so that he could come for me later? I immediately decided not to tell Mutti about the incident. How would we survive if Dieter and I were no longer allowed to go begging?

Kaetchen and her sons returned home late that afternoon. "Emmy and Lianchen, let me tell you about our great God," she said with a sparkle in her deeply sunken eyes. "When we arrived at the Polish headquarters, they told me that all buckets and scrubbing brushes were already in use. Why would they round up more women than they had buckets? That was very strange indeed and made me wonder. We were then led into the very room where we used to conduct our church services before the Nazis turned it into their headquarters. When I was confronted by five stern-looking officers, I silently prayed, 'Lord, take control and keep me strong.'"

Two of the officers spoke German rather well. They fired question after question at me about our family, our occupation, our relatives, our home, and our plans for the future. They asked if I knew where Wilhelm is and if we have a radio here in the house. They even interrogated Hanno. Did he see a radio at our house this week or did he hear one? Then, they continued asking me questions. Have we made contact with anyone in the West? Do I know of German soldiers hiding somewhere? Did we ever hide soldiers? Are any Nazis at our house? How many people are living at our house? What are their names and ages and what are their occupations? What is our religion? And then they reverted to the question of the radio and repeated many others. But, Emmychen, I know that our God strengthened me. My mind did not tire even after all those hours of strain."

"Praise His name," Mutti responded joyfully. "Our God is wonderful." Then, suddenly, she had a puzzled look on her face. "Is it possible that our quiet neighbor from across the street was spying on us? Did she turn us in?"

One really had to wonder. Why did she have food when everyone else in town was starving? Was food her payment for spying? "But where would she get the idea that we possessed a radio?" Mutti continued. "That was taken by the first troops! Where would we get one now?"

"I don't know." Kaetchen sank into a chair. "But that question came up more than any other and made me wonder, too—oh, Emmy! Do you think our neighbor is tiptoeing past our window in the evening, and when she hears us sing and talk to the Lord, she thinks that is a radio?" Both of the mothers exploded with laughter when they realized that it could have been possible.

The next Sunday afternoon someone really did creep up outside our house. Tap! Tap! Someone quietly rapped on the living room window. A peek through the curtains revealed a kind-looking man with a white beard. Who could he be? When Onkel Emil opened the door just a crack, the stranger asked if this was the home of Ernst Lehmann, the preacher.

"Yes, it is," he answered.

"I am a preacher, too," he said in German. "Is Ernst Lehmann at home?"

"Yes, he is. Come in," responded Onkel Emil, inviting him into the living room.

After introductions, the old preacher tearfully began to tell us about his family. "The Russians have taken my wife and my six children to Siberia. They are probably at hard labor there in the coal mines, along with many thousands of Germans and other Polish people. I was too sickly and of no use to them in the slave labor camps; so they forced me to leave my home and come here to help them occupy Germany. I know that God brought me to Lippehne for a reason, even though that reason is still unknown to me. I am sorrowful for my wife and children, and that is why my hair and beard are white. There are a few Polish believers here in town and a Russian who is a believer. We meet on Sunday mornings, just one block from here, at my house. Please come and fellowship with us. But please be careful not to give our meetings away."

We had a time of fellowship and prayer before our new friend left. The following morning he returned with two of the most wonderful gifts: a loaf of white bread and a small piece of margarine.

In spite of the unexpected blessing of food, Mutti seemed somewhat discouraged that day. Early in the afternoon she had an unusual request. "Schaefle, can you and Dieter pull me to the lake in the handwagon today?"

"Of course, Mutti, but why do you want to go to the lake?" I thought immediately of the mother who, along with her children, committed suicide by drowning in that same lake.

"I just have to find out if the cool water of the lake will give my legs some relief from pain." Mutti had been suffering much lately. Her legs were so swollen and blistered from near-starvation that it was difficult for her to walk at all.

With Mutti, Udo, and Marlies all loaded into the wagon, off we went. The July sun had us perspiring in the short time before we arrived at the lake. Tiny ripples danced across the water today, and the breeze felt wonderfully refreshing. Mutti gathered her long, black skirt, slowly seated herself on the small dock, and lowered her legs into the water. The rest of us quickly removed our shoes and socks and did the same. Because Udo's legs were too short, I had to hold him down over the edge of the dock to reach the water. Dieter, of course, tried to catch some crabs, but they were considerably faster than he was. Udo's and Marlies's happy chatter was almost as beautiful as the songs of the birds, and I noticed signs of both joy and pain on Mutti's face as she watched her children relishing those few moments in nature.

"Do your legs feel better in the water, Dieter?" Mutti asked.

"They feel much, much better, Mutti. Can we come down here every day?"

"I wish we could, my son. The water feels soothing on my legs, too. We'll try to come again if you children are able to pull such a heavy load."

Sunday morning finally came—the day that we were to go to the Polish preacher's house. The church service started at 9:30 A.M. We had made plans the previous night to try to make the journey as inconspicuously as possible. Onkel Lehmann would be the first to leave our house at 8:30 A.M. Ten or fifteen minutes later Kaetchen and her sons would meander down the street. Mutti, Udo, and Marlies would remain at home. It would have been impossible for Mutti to walk that far. Onkel Emil, Dieter, and I would start our stroll ten minutes before church time.

If any of us spotted any soldiers, Russian or Polish, we were not to enter the preacher's house, but instead just walk right past. Bibles were to be hidden under coats and jackets.

Thankfully, everything moved as precisely as planned. When we arrived at "church," we were all relieved and grateful that all from our house had made the walk in safety.

It was difficult for me to distinguish one Polish lady from another at church. They all wore babushkas and their round, wrinkled faces looked old and weather-beaten. Their eyes sparkled, though, and their mouths were drawn into smiles. The presence of a Russian soldier in the room gave me a scary feeling. When I first saw him, I looked quickly away, fighting panic. When I dared glance at him again, my fears were somewhat calmed by the kind-looking expression on his face.

The Polish preacher opened the service with a prayer of which I understood nothing but "Amen." Then he began the song service with the hymn "Amazing Grace." Everyone sang in a hushed voice and in his native language. The subdued singing continued until tears filled the eyes of everyone in the room.

"Please read Psalm 91 for us, Pastor Lehmann," the Polish preacher said in German.

After Onkel Lehmann finished reading the whole psalm, he reviewed the promises God has given us in that psalm alone: He will deliver us; He will cover us with His feathers; He will give His angels charge over us; He will answer if we call on Him. As he spoke, everyone's head nodded in agreement. Did they understand German? I wondered. Bible readings in the Russian and Polish languages followed the message. Then everybody began to sing again. It was such a strange, yet warm, feeling to realize that voices in three different languages could sing about the same Lord. Sometimes I had imagined what it would be like to attend a service in a foreign country. I had wondered if people would worship in the same manner we did in Germany. Or was God really worshiped in other countries? How could He listen to prayers in so many different languages?

Suddenly a strange realization struck me. We no longer lived in Germany! We lived in a foreign country! Our government was both Polish and Russian, but no longer German. What country did that make the soil on which we stood? My thoughts had strayed while the adults in our service were taking turns praying. As they whispered their prayers, many of them were weeping. When the soldier prayed, however, I immediately felt anger welling up in me. Not until I reminded myself that he was a believer in the Lord Jesus, too, did a stillness take over my heart. All Russians must not be bad. Jesus died for him just as He did for every single human being on earth; therefore, my thoughts toward him must be kind and loving.

After a few more songs—all of them were sung from memory— we closed with the hymn "Blest Be the Tie That Binds." Everyone in the small room formed a human chain by holding hands. I was sitting next to the Russian, but I couldn't make myself take his hand. He reached over and took my hand anyway, gently placing it in his as we continued singing.

... our hearts in Christian love;
The fellowship of kindred minds
Is like to that above.

That night was unusually calm. Everyone except Onkel Lehmann felt better after a peaceful rest. He wasn't feeling well, but planned to go to work anyway. During that day, most of our thoughts were still on the church service of the day before.

"What a blessing to worship with other believers," Kaetchen said to Mutti as we scrubbed laundry in the kitchen. "One could sense the Lord's Spirit in that small room. We could hardly understand one another, but there was no doubt in my mind that we were one in the Lord. The blood of our Lord reached into Poland and Russia, 'that whosoever believeth in him should not perish, but have everlasting life.' I am so glad I asked for forgiveness of sins as a young person and invited Christ into my life. How would we cope today if He weren't our Comforter and Helper?"

"Of course, Kaetchen, I feel exactly the way you do. At times, however, doubts set in. We try to live pure before Him with His help, and we love the Lord. Why, then, do we have to go through such difficult times? Why can't we fill the stomachs of our little children? Then again I am just overwhelmed by the fact that we are still alive. When I realize that this alone is a miracle, my fainting heart revives itself and I just love Him more."

"Emmy, I think we'll experience even greater miracles. Can you imagine today how we will be united with our husbands? I can't, but I know that we will be. We must be faithful to our Lord during our struggles and not waver. We must not turn from Him as Israel did, time after time. He has bought us with a price, His precious blood. Nothing we go through today can compare to His suffering. He understands everything we are going through, and He will give us the strength to come forth as gold, as Job did."

"Schaefle," Mutti interrupted the train of thought, "don't wring the underwear too much. It might tear. Instead of wringing the water out, just squeeze it out with your hands, all right?"

"I have already been doing that with the socks."

"Only the Lord knows when we will be able to purchase new clothing. In the meantime we have to be very careful with the few things we have."

"Aren't our little ones pure joy, Emmychen? Look how nicely they are playing in the courtyard." Kaetchen motioned for Mutti to look out of the kitchen window. "The sun is so wonderful for all of them. Even Hanno's cheeks are getting a little color."

"We should be more thankful for our children," Mutti admitted. "They don't complain, even though they are always hungry. They get along so well with one another. Isn't it amazing that they never run out of things to play, even though they have so few toys? We are truly blessed women, aren't we, Kaetchen?"

In the evening Onkel Lehmann slowly entered the kitchen with his little chunk of bread.

"It is a truly ridiculous job to guard furniture at the railroad station because we know it will never be shipped to Russia. The elements have their claim on it rather than our enemies. Since it is a job I am required to do, however, I should not complain, in spite of the fact that it wore me out completely today. If you don't mind, I'll go to bed early," he said. "You can divide my morsel of bread between you."

Kaetchen's eyes followed her father with a look of concern as she watched him shuffle into the living room.

"Vati must be sick," she said sadly.

The next morning, as Dieter and I prepared to go on our food hunt, Kaetchen slowly climbed upstairs with the sad news that Onkel Lehmann and five-year-old Hanno were very ill. "They both have diarrhea and don't feel well. Let's pray that no one else will get sick."

Dieter and I ventured to the far side of town to visit Onkel Lehmann's big garden. We found the gate wide open and the hedge on either side of the gate scraggly and in need of pruning. The little summer house had been vandalized and several of the windows were broken. We searched through the reeds for the boat, but it had vanished. The vegetable rows, which last year had been neatly planted with carrots, beets, lettuce, beans, and cabbage, now resembled a large weed patch. The red and yellow currants and the gooseberries promised to be a good crop in a few weeks. A few marigold seeds had defied winter's cold and planted themselves near the long garden path. They were blooming beautifully.

"Dieter, if it would not have been so dangerous a few months ago, we could have come to put some vegetable seeds into the ground. Onkel Lehmann saved his seeds, but now it is too late for this year. We'll have to come back when the berries and apples are ripe and get some. Wouldn't it be wonderful to eat fruit right now?"

"Don't talk about it, please! That is not fair to my stomach," Dieter pleaded.

"Do you hear all that noise at the public beach? There must be quite a few soldiers at the beach restaurant. Why don't we go and see? They might give us something to eat."

We decided to take the narrow path along the reeds to the swimming area. Only one garden separated Onkel Lehmann's property from the beach. When the narrow path and reeds ended and we were out in the open, we noticed that the white sand was cluttered with olive green uniforms. Nude soldiers were swimming, wrestling in the water, and jumping off the diving boards. I felt terribly embarrassed, and we quickly crossed the wide sand strip toward the restaurant.

The restaurant had always been a beautiful spot. The tables had been neatly covered with white linen tablecloths, and the wooden chairs never seemed to leave a mark on the highly polished parquet floor. The huge windows that overlooked the beach area and the hills on the other side of the lake were constantly sparkling. Folk music played softly as people enjoyed meals or just pastries and coffee.

As we went closer, Dieter pointed out all the broken windows. The main door was wide open and my heart was crushed when I saw the awful change that had taken place since last fall. The floor of the huge dining hall was littered with cigarette butts, garbage, beer bottles, and broken glass. Furniture pieces and table and chair legs were lying here and there with the table tops and seats nowhere in sight. It made me wonder if Lippehne would ever again be the way I remembered it.

Onkel Lehmann was not able to go to work again the next day. He had a fever accompanied by chills, and Hanno appeared to have the same problem. Since it seemed to be a contagious disease, we were no longer allowed to go downstairs to visit or play. Our small quarters became even more confining with the first floor off limits. Mutti sewed in our room, and the four of us children spent more time in the attic. Two of the walls were slanted and two small sky lights could be propped open with a notched metal bar. When we wanted to see what was transpiring on the other side of the street, we just climbed on a chair, opened the hatch, and stuck our heads out. Udo and Marlies were upset when they realized they were too small to be able to look out.

Two soldiers came to our house to inquire why Onkel Lehmann had not reported for work. "When they saw him and Hanno in-bed," Kaetchen told us from the base of the steps, "they quickly covered their mouths with their hands and said: 'Typhoid, typhoid,' and almost stumbled over each other to get out of the door. That is a disease of poor sanitation and hygiene, isn't it? How can that be, Emmychen? Everything is clean here. How do they know what disease this is by just looking at the sick ones?" We didn't know the answer to that, but a whole week passed without soldiers coming to the house and harassing us. Our first peaceful week since January!

"The soldiers must have passed the word around," Mutti told me, "that there is a contagious disease at the Lehmanns' house. That should explain why we haven't been molested by them." Suddenly her face lit up and her eyes twinkled as she seemed to have come upon something pleasant.

"I have an idea, a great idea. If we wish to have another peaceful week, we'll just nail a poster on the front door with the word TYPHOID on it." Quickly she informed Onkel Emil and Kaetchen of her brainstorm, and both of them agreed with it wholeheartedly.

A short time later, the green front door had a heavy, white piece of paper fastened to it, bearing the name of the deadly disease.

9
The Deadly Disease

Onkel Lehmann's fever rose, and so did Hanno's. It was almost a blessing that neither of them had an appetite because things seemed hopeless with Kaetchen's breadwinner laid up. She was no longer bubbly and joyful. Two of her men, as she called them, were sick, and there was no doctor in town and no medicine for whatever their illness might be. We couldn't pray or sing together anymore—everything was so different. I had never thought that I would miss the sick ones so much. Gloom was settling into all of our hearts, for we realized that both of them were growing steadily weaker.

"There is nothing we can do but pray," Mutti told us. "The Lord can make them well in an instant, if He so chooses. He can heal as He did in Bible times. We don't know what His plan is, and often we don't understand it, but we must trust Him to do what He deems best."

"But how can it be best for my friend Hanno to be so sick?" Dieter asked.

"I don't know, Son. I don't know. Only the Lord knows."

The Polish preacher was almost out of breath the next day when he came to the house to tell Kaetchen that he just heard of the reopening of the Lippehne hospital. It was staffed by Polish doctors and nurses, and he planned to go immediately and see if Onkel Lehmann and Hanno could be admitted. Half an hour later he returned to inform Kaetchen that there was room for both of them. Kaetchen quickly readied the handwagon and placed her weak father in it. He had a very high fever now.

"Please pray that Vati will be able to withstand that fifteen-minute, bumpy ride in the handwagon," she pleaded with us as we waved goodbye through our tears. "He is a very sick man."

We listened to the rattle of the handwagon as the metal bands of the wagon hit the cobblestones.

Tired and worn out, Kaetchen returned for the second load, her oldest son. Was it my imagination or had I detected some gray hair peeking out from under her black scarf? She hadn't had gray hair two weeks ago.

Marlies and Udo were tugging at me. They wanted me to play with them, but I just didn't feel like playing. Sadness had engulfed me, too. Two of our family members were in the hospital! Who would be next? Would we all get sick? Would we all die? When we heard the noisy handwagon clanking down the street again, we knew it was Kaetchen. Dieter and I rushed to push the iron bar from the small barnyard door and help her pull in the wagon.

"You take care of the children, Schaefle. I have to go and talk to Kaetchen," Mutti told me.

I was trying my best to entertain my brothers and sister, while at the same time listen for Mutti's footsteps. A long time went by before she finally came upstairs again. Her eyes looked red and puffy. She must have been crying.

"Kaetchen can go and visit Onkel Lehmann and Hanno at the hospital every day until they are well enough to return home," she reported.

"Can I go and see my friend Hanno, too?"

"No, Dieter, children are not allowed to visit the hospital."

"With whom can I play now in my spare time? Udo and Marlies are too little. Vilmar is too little. Liane is too busy. Here I am now, all by myself."

"Come here, you little curly-head," Mutti said and opened her arms. "Let me give you a hug. So you are feeling sorry for yourself, are you?"

"I do. I have no friend. My friend is in the hospital."

"You don't have to feel lonely, Dieter. You still have all of us. Do you know what, Son? I have a marvelous idea, an idea I think you'll like."

"What is that?"

"I have an assignment that will be just perfect for you."

"What is it, Mutti? What is it?"

"I think an eight-year-old young man would make an excellent teacher for the little ones. I hereby nominate you, Herr Guddat, as teacher of these students. Use the old mattress there as the classroom area and set things up the way you like. Teach your students the alphabet and teach them some of the things you learned at school. You might also want to check them on their knowledge of poetry. By that I mean," her voice dropped to a whisper, "the poems for Vati's homecoming."

"Yes, Mutti, yes! I'll start right now." A few minutes later, when Mutti and I peeked into the attic through the cracked door, the only school in Lippehne was in session and every student most attentive.

Kaetchen was very discouraged the next day after she returned home from the hospital. "Emmy," she said, "we must continually pray for my men. The diagnosis was that both of them have typhoid and have to be in isolation because the disease is highly contagious. I am not permitted to even set one foot in the hospital. I have to go there daily, however, and pick up their soiled laundry, which the nurses will place at the entrance. Both of them are too weak to use the bathroom, and the hospital staff does not launder anything. The Lord will have to give me an extra measure of strength to help me do that job without getting sick myself."

The continued nights of peace helped all of us to gather physical and emotional strength. Even Kaetchen was able to endure the daily stress of walking back and forth to the hospital and doing the laundry for the two sick ones.

"I saw my son today, Emmychen." She returned one day with a shadow of a smile. "I found a tall ladder near the hospital, dragged it there, and leaned it against the window on the second floor. Emmychen, I wanted to cry when I saw Hanno, but I could not let him see my tears. My poor son is just a shadow. I waved to him, but he couldn't wave back. His eyes are black-looking and sunken in. He just stared at the window. Oh, how I wanted to hold him in my arms and comfort him! I saw Vati through the window also. He is on the first floor. He is very bad, too, but he at least raised his arm a little to wave back to me."

The next day Kaetchen pushed herself into the house, bent over, sobbing, and exhausted. When we saw her in the hallway in such despair, no one said a word or asked a question. We all knew that something terrible had happened. Mutti embraced her and let her cry.

"I wish I would have never had to hear those words," she stammered: " 'Frau Mecklenburg, your father will live, but your son will die.' This is what the doctor told me. Why, Lord, why? I have already lost one son and now You want another? Why?" Her frail body was wracked with pain, and there was no one who could help her today. All of Mutti's efforts were in vain.

Onkel Emil really struggled that night to have everybody join him in our time of devotions. Only Marlies and Udo were willing to help him with the singing. Quietly they sang:

God is love, He set me free.
God is love, He loves ev'n me.
That's why I repeat it again,
God is love, He loves me.

Kaetchen wept softly as Onkel Emil led a few more songs. Then, leafing through the book of Psalms, he read to her:

Wait on the Lord: be of good courage, and he shall strengthen thine heart: wait, I say, on the Lord. . . . The Lord is my strength and my shield; my heart trusted in him, and I am helped. . . . I sought the Lord, and he heard me, and delivered me from all my fears.

Then we all quoted the Twenty-third Psalm in unison.

"Kaetchen," Onkel Emil continued, "we are unable to comfort you tonight. We wish we could help you, but we have no idea how. There is only One who can still your soul, and that is the Lord Jesus Christ. Rest in Him completely! I know some of what you are going through. Mally and I lost our only son in the war, as you know. We've known the sorrow, but I am still no expert on it. When I look back, I think there were really only two things that helped us in the loss of our only son: knowing that the Lord still cared and was still in control, and knowing people were praying for us. Our friends wanted to help us, too, but there was nothing more they could do to ease our pain."

As the prayers ascended that night, I found myself constantly tormented by thoughts of death and dying. Except for the little ones, everyone wept, but when we wished each other a restful and peaceful night, Kaetchen once again had that lovely smile on her slender face.

Sometime later, I came wide awake without knowing why. It must have been the middle of the night. Why is Udo crying? Marlies was awake and so was Mutti. Then I realized someone was relentlessly beating on the shutters of the downstairs windows.

"Woman, open up! Open up! Need suit for dancing! Your father in hospital said you give suit."

The racket continued, and the same command again came upstairs from the street. Onkel Emil hit his head on the slanted wall of the attic as he tried to scramble out of bed to get down-stairs. He angrily told the two men to leave.

"It is midnight," he shouted. "Go away!"

"No, Emil," Kaetchen said, "here is Vati's suit. Just give it to them." Then I heard the front door opening and someone saying:

"Thank you. Thank you." Abruptly, calm and silence returned to our house.

A couple of days later, Dieter and I figured that the berries at Onkel Lehmann's farm should be ripe. Excitedly we hurried across town to Onkel Lehmann's garden. As we carried our little buckets, I envisioned how it would be to pick currants and gooseberries and take them home for everyone to enjoy. The summer weather had been gorgeous. How wonderful the warm sun felt as we meandered along the lake. Only a few puffy clouds were sailing gently across the sky. The birds chirped, diving in and out of the tree tops with leafy rustling. I thought it must be nice to be a bird and have so much fun and nothing to worry about.

The tall, stately linden trees along the promenade bathed in the golden warmth of the sun. The still lake was a perfect mirror of all we saw. It was so peaceful.

"I wish I could know the names of some of the birds, Liane. I like that beautiful song. Let's sneak up on the little one over there in the grass and see if we can catch it." Dieter began to tiptoe through the park lawn, but the little bird must have been watching, too. It soared into the blue sky before Dieter could even approach it.

"Do the Polish people like flowers, Liane?"

"Yes, Dieter. Everybody likes flowers. Why do you ask?"

"Because I don't see any flowers in the gardens this year, only wild daisies."

"You know, I hadn't even noticed that, but I think you are right. They probably didn't have time to plant any because they are just getting settled here in Lippehne."

It hardly surprised me to find the gate to Onkel Lehmann's garden wide open again when we arrived, but Dieter was quicker than I was to notice more.

"We closed the gate when we were here the last time, didn't we? Now will you just look over there!" His voice rose in disappointment as we passed through the gate. "Can you believe it?"

"Can I believe what, Dieter?"

"Look at the berry bushes over there! The berries are gone. Somebody stole them! This is Onkel Lehmann's garden. Why do they do that to us?"

My heart sank. It was true. All the bushes were picked clean.

"Dieter, I think this is no longer Onkel Lehmann's garden. It belongs to everybody now. The Germans don't seem to own anything anymore."

"Maybe we can find a few berries at the very bottom of the bushes. Let's check." Our search was in vain, however.

"The birds must have gotten those that may have been overlooked by the thieves." I could hear the disappointment in my own voice.

"We came too late," Dieter said with tears in his eyes. "Maybe we can beat the thieves to the apples. They are still small and hard."

"Yes, let's try that. We'll ask Kaetchen when they are supposed to be ripe. But now, let's gather sticks on our way home, so we won't go back empty-handed. I think we should do some begging, too."

On our way back home, we gathered sticks on the promenade. Our arms were almost full, but we were still scouting. Suddenly, out of nowhere, a huge horse appeared, charging toward us with a thunder of hooves.

"Let's duck in here, Dieter! Fast!" I dropped my sticks and pulled Dieter into the entrance of a farmyard which we were just passing. We hid behind the gate.

"That was close," Dieter whispered as the horse tore past. "We could have been killed." So relieved were we that we almost missed the new danger. Barely in time I saw the figure moving up behind us.

"Watch out, Dieter. Run! Run!" The farmer's wife swung a broom and came running after us, yelling and screaming. Dieter dropped his sticks, and we ran as fast as we could, angry Polish words following us. When we finally reached the park, we saw nothing: no horse and no farmer's wife. The trees still basked in the sun and the birds still played hide and seek. Starved and empty-handed, we arrived at home.

The nurse at the hospital informed Kaetchen that both Onkel Lehmann and Hanno were being given one slice of bread each day, but neither of them would eat.

"I told Hanno through the closed window: 'When you start eating, I'll come and take you home.' It was terrible, Emmychen, he only stared at me and didn't respond at all. He doesn't seem to care about coming home. I feel so helpless. What can I do to help my son?"

"I have no idea, Kaetchen. Did you try again to get into his room?"

"Yes, I did, just today, but they still won't give me permission. Typhoid is too contagious."

"I can't help you, Kaetchen. All I can do is pray, and I am doing that."

"Thank you, Emmychen, thank you. I know there is nothing anyone can do. Only our Lord can ease the pain."

"Yes, what would we do without Him?"

"Emmychen, I want to help you a bit. I'll take care of your little ones while Dieter and Liane take you to the lake to cool your sores. Would you like me to do that? I sense that you are in a lot of pain."

"Oh, thank you, Kaetchen. That sounds like a marvelous idea. Thank you for your suggestion."

"But be very careful. A young Russian soldier followed me all the way to the hospital this morning. Please be careful. I'll be praying for you all."

It was very difficult for Mutti to walk now. Her legs were always swollen. We took her to the lake as often as possible, but when she slowly slid off the handwagon we had to help her down to the dock and take off her shoes. Dieter's bandages would be off in seconds. He also got relief from the cool water. The sun bathed everything in its warm glow, even the cemetery on the other side of the lake, so that the tombstones and catacombs looked pleasant among the green trees.

"Mutti, what happened to all those who died by drowning since we lost our freedom? Did anyone bury them? And the man's body which Dieter and I saw in the lake a few months ago, what happened to it?"

"I have no idea, Schaefle. I presume that the German work crews probably buried them somewhere. Those who died in the treks from Eastern Germany were not so fortunate. They were just dragged into the ditches along the roads. Nobody had time to worry about the dead. Staying alive and escaping the enemy were everyone's main concerns. Thousands will never know the final resting place of their loved ones. Just think of all those people whom the Russians mercilessly crushed with their tanks! No one knows the miseries the German people have suffered—any more than we know what they will continue to suffer."

"Hitler was shaking his fist at the face of God, and all of us are paying for that now. I read somewhere that he once said that after he had won the war, he would sit on a throne and would make all the preachers crawl under it on their knees. You see, Schaefle, God had to prevent that. No one mistreats or plans to mistreat God's people without having to pay the consequences. God is a just God, and I feel He is pouring out His judgment on Germany."

"But we have loved the Lord, Mutti! You and Vati, all our grandparents, and great-grandparents have been believers in the Lord. Why then do we all have to suffer? And Onkel Lehmann? He loves the Lord with all his heart."

"I know what you are saying, and I don't have the answers to your questions. All I know is that God is still on the throne, He still loves us, and no matter what happens we must believe that and trust Him. His Word says, 'I will never leave thee nor forsake thee.' Isn't that a comforting promise?"

"Yes, it is."

"Help! Someone help!" Dieter called excitedly. "I caught one. I caught a crab! Where can I put it?" With his right hand on the back of the crab he splashed toward us. The little animal squirmed and the claws flopped back and forth in search of something to hold on to. "I should have brought my bucket. We could have taken it home and cooked it."

"I didn't think about that either, Dieter," Mutti said sadly. "But you are fast today to have caught this one."

"Can you hold it on your lap, Mutti, when we pull you home? I will show you how to hold it so it won't bite you."

"I guess I could do that."

We arrived at home refreshed in body and spirit. For dinner that night Dieter enjoyed one mouthful of crab meat.

10
Onkel Lehmann

It was the sixth day of September and Kaetchen didn't have to tell us. When she returned from the hospital we knew that one of her men had died. We could see that her whole being was torn with grief.

"He went to be with his Lord this morning. He no longer has to suffer. Our Vati is safe in the arms of Jesus." Mutti helped Kaetchen to the couch in the living room where the two friends sat down, held hands, and wept.

Onkel Lehmann died? But the doctor said that he would live! My mind whirled. Our best friend was gone. I couldn't comprehend it. Yes, I had seen a lot of death, but death took on a different meaning that day. It was Onkel Lehmann's death.

I was trying to keep the children entertained, but Dieter had to take over for me because I was no longer able to function. Sadness gripped my heart and wouldn't let go of me. We would never see Onkel Lehmann again? The kind, gentle man! He always lived close to the Lord. Whenever he prayed, I had thought that he must be standing directly before God. He had such a love for people and helped them in many ways, but his greatest concern had been for their souls. "You must be born again," he told the neighbors who sought refuge at our house. "One way leads to heaven and one way leads to hell. You alone have to decide where you want to spend eternity. Our loving God does not force anyone to accept the gift of His Son. You must reach out and take it."

What would we do now without Onkel Lehmann's prayers for us? How would Kaetchen live without him? How would we all exist without him? Just to have been in Onkel Lehmann's presence when we were in difficulty had always soothed us.

"Onkel Lehmann went to heaven today, children," Kaetchen said as she gathered the little ones around her. "He went to be with Jesus. Isn't that wonderful? He loved the Lord Jesus very much and couldn't wait to see Him. And now he sees Him as clearly as I see all of you and you see me. We will miss Opi terribly here on earth, but we can't be sad. Heaven is a far better place than anywhere on earth. It is much more beautiful, and there is *nothing* better than seeing Jesus every day."

"Will he see Ulli, too, Mutti?" Vilmar asked excitedly.

"Yes, Vilmar, Opi is right there with your brother."

"Oh, that's good. Then Ulli won't be so alone."

"Yes," Kaetchen said. "Opi will keep him company until we get there." Then Vilmar pulled Udo by the hand and both wanted to dash off to play.

"Come here now, Vilmar," Kaetchen told him and caught him by the arm. "Come, sit on my lap." I noticed that she was almost too weak to pick up her two-year-old.

"Hanno is still very sick, and I would like all of us to pray for him right now."

"Will he go to heaven, too?" Marlies asked.

"I don't know, Pittimaus. We want him to stay with us here on earth, but maybe Jesus wants him to be in heaven, too. We'll just have to let Jesus decide. He knows what is best."

The next morning Dieter and I went to the lake to get evergreen branches from some of the hemlock and spruce trees. After several trips our arms were scratched up, but Mutti had enough greens to make two wreaths. The funeral service was to be the next day. Two of Onkel Lehmann's old carpenter friends and co-workers came to the house to tell Kaetchen that they had built a casket for him.

"We could find only a few boards; so we had to build it very low," they remarked.

106

"You have no idea what your expression of friendship means to me," Kaetchen told them. "You are so kind. Nothing I could say would adequately tell how I feel about what you have done. Thank you very much—I will ask our Lord to reward you richly."

"I wonder, though," Kaetchen continued, "if you know that Germans are not allowed to be buried in a casket."

"We know that. But not even in death will we permit our friend to be humiliated and embarrassed by our enemies. We will not stand for that no matter what the consequences will be for us. We will stop by tomorrow morning to pick up your handwagon and then meet you at the hospital. Auf Wiedersehen."

"This is a true miracle, Kaetchen. Our Onkel Lehmann will be taken to the cemetery in a casket," Mutti rejoiced with tears in her eyes, "and he will not be made a laughing stock. Praise the Lord. He has again showed Himself faithful to His children."

Our Polish preacher friend walked alongside us to the cemetery. Mutti's legs had improved enough for her to limp slowly with the aid of a cane. Nobody talked, not even the little ones. Did they understand the reason for this outing?

It was a warm, sunny September day, and the long walk to the outskirts of town was sad, but oddly refreshing as well. No one seemed to think about the enemy possibly lurking behind a house or tree. Our thoughts were on heaven that day, and we must have been oblivious to fear.

The closed casket was placed next to the open earth in the new part of the cemetery, a green meadow. A wall of small shrubs sheltered us from the breeze. The preacher and Onkel Emil each took one of the wreaths and laid it on the roughly hewn, board casket. Onkel Emil then began to lead us in singing some of Onkel Lehmann's favorite hymns.

Safe in the arms of Jesus, safe on His gentle breast,
There by His love o'ershaded, sweetly my soul shall rest.
Hark! 'Tis the voice of angels, borne in a song to me,
Over the fields of Glory, over the jasper sea.
Safe in the arms of Jesus, safe on His gentle breast.
There by His love o'ershaded, sweetly my soul shall rest.

Then we all continued singing softly:

When peace, like a river, attendeth my way,
When sorrows like sea billows roll;
Whatever my lot, Thou hast taught me to say,

"It is well, it is well with my soul."
And, Lord, haste the day when the faith shall be sight,
The clouds be rolled back as a scroll,
The trump shall resound and the Lord shall descend,
"Even so,"—it is well with my soul.

The preacher sang all the songs in his native language. Onkel Emil then pulled Mutti's Bible out from under his coat, opened it to I Thessalonians and began reading from chapter 4, verses 13 to 18:

But I would not have you to be ignorant, brethren, concerning them which are asleep, that ye sorrow not, even as others which have no hope. For if we believe that Jesus died and rose again, even so them also which sleep in Jesus will God bring with him. For this we say unto you by the word of the Lord, that we which are alive and remain unto the coming of the Lord shall not prevent them which are asleep. For the Lord himself shall descend from heaven with a shout, with the voice of the archangel, and with the trump of God: and the dead in Christ shall rise first: Then we which are alive and remain shall be caught up together with them in the clouds, to meet the Lord in the air: and so shall we ever be with the Lord. Wherefore comfort one another with these words.

While the adults listened attentively to the Bible reading, I watched Kaetchen. Her face was drawn and sad, but her eyes were dry. She was constantly looking upward. Did she see her father in heaven?

Onkel Emil supported himself on his cane while the pastor read some Bible passages in Polish. Then we continued singing the hymns Onkel Lehmann had most often requested. Prayers of thanksgiving were offered for Onkel Lehmann's life, for his walk with the Lord, for his witness and example he had been to others, for the end of his suffering, for his kindness and love for others, and for his being at rest now and in the presence of his Lord.

As we stood there celebrating Onkel Lehmann's graduation, I noticed a young-looking couple walking slowly toward a casket and an open grave only about fifteen feet from us. I had wondered about that grave when we first arrived at the cemetery, for there were no flowers and no people, just a casket and the open grave. Our service was almost over when the lady opened the other casket, threw herself across it, and screamed as I have never heard anyone scream. Kneeling down in the grass, she leaned over to kiss the body, mingling her wailing with words we did not understand. When we were finished with our service, we all moved over to the couple and stood in silence with bowed heads. A young boy about my age lay in the plain casket. He looked handsome in his white suit, white shirt, and black shoes. Someone my age dead? So young? It could have been me, I knew, but as I stood there, my only thought was of whether or not he had been prepared for eternity.

The preacher reached down and placed his hand on the lady's shoulder. Her whole body was shaking. He said something to her, took the husband's right hand, enclosed it in both of his, and spoke to him. How I wished we could help this couple and tell them of God's peace, but we couldn't. The woman's hysterical screams followed us for a long time after we left the cemetery.

After that day, surviving without being able to purchase food became an even greater problem. Other than Onkel Emil's watery soup, we had no means of getting provisions. Mutti still sewed, and sometimes her pay was bread and lard.

"Emmychen, on the way home from the hospital I picked these apples. I don't know if anyone owns the garden now or not, but I was just too hungry. I had to get something to eat. Here are some apples for you and the children."

Mutti's mouth was beginning to water, I could see that, and so was mine.

"Apples! Fruit! Kaetchen! You, the pastor's wife, took apples, or shall we say, stole apples? I can't believe it. You really did that?" Mutti teased with a twinkle in her eyes.

Kaetchen looked at the floor. "For all we know, Emmychen, the owner of that tree may not even be alive now. I do feel uncomfortable about it, though, and I've already asked the Lord to forgive me. The Lord forgave King David when he ate the showbread—He understands our hunger pangs."

"He was hungry, too, when He walked on this earth." Mutti consoled her friend. "How would He otherwise ever know and understand what we are going through?"

One day the neighbor across the street informed us that some of the railroad tracks were repaired, and trains were reaching Berlin regularly now. We could probably board one and leave for Germany. She had heard of several people who had left for the West.

"Are you planning to leave, too?" Mutti asked her.

"No, I don't plan to leave Lippehne. I like it here. I have a good life."

After that conversation, it seemed that no one at home talked of anything else except escape.

We couldn't tell any outsider about our plans. We had to leave secretly. Of course, we could take along only what we were able to carry, so preparing everything in detail was of utmost importance. The adults spent much time debating about the move, but on one thing they all agreed. The timing of everything would have to depend on Hanno's recovery. There appeared to be a slight improvement in him, and we thought he might be released from the hospital in another week.

"We must pray hard for that," Mutti said. "We also must pray more diligently for food, because without food Hanno can't regain his strength. And if he is too weak to walk, we can't leave, because there is no one strong enough to carry him."

The Russians had somehow learned of our secret meetings, and our church services had been forbidden. If the group should defy headquarters' orders, the punishment for all would be most severe, the pastor had been told. Our emotional survival was again being challenged and tested—again we had to live without fellowship. We needed that warmth in Christ. We all wondered why the Lord allowed us to be so isolated.

On Sunday we all walked to the cemetery to visit Onkel Lehmann's grave. His body had such a peaceful resting place. The earth above the grave had settled since our last visit and the wreaths still looked fresh. After quietly standing there for a while, we softly began singing some of his favorite songs:

> When all my labors and trials are o'er,
> And I am safe on that beautiful shore,
> Just to be near the dear Lord I adore
> Will through the ages be glory for me.
> Oh, that will be glory for me.
> When by His grace I shall look on His face,
> That will be glory, be glory for me.

Onkel Emil asked us all to bow our heads and close our eyes. He then began to praise the Lord for the beautiful, peaceful day and asked Him to protect Vati, Kaetchen's husband, and his wife. Then, except for the little ones, we all prayed the Lord's Prayer in whispering tones.

"Kaetchen," Mutti said, "we have faith in the Lord, but what does our faith do for us? What does it matter whether I believe in the Lord or not? We have absolutely nothing to feed our children today, and look at our godless enemies. They are strong and healthy—and our children are sick and covered with boils. They don't seem to believe in anything, and we believe in the Creator of the universe. So why is God so silent? Why must we suffer so? Why is your son so ill?"

I had never heard Mutti express doubts. Was it really Mutti who was talking that way?

"Emmychen, I have never heard you talk like this before." Kaetchen was concerned. "It seems to me that the devil is really pulling you down. That definitely isn't the voice of someone who loves the Lord dearly! Please don't let Satan get hold of your heart. You know that the Lord is far greater, and He will miraculously provide for our children. Emmychen, you must not talk this way! Our children need to see our strength, our true strength, and not the onslaughts of the devil. If we let our faith weaken, we have nothing to live for and will never get out of Lippehne. So, Emmychen, 'be strong and of a good courage. Be not afraid neither be thou dismayed; for the Lord, thy God is with thee whithersoever thou goest.' "

The two friends stood in silence, until Mutti began to weep.

"Oh, Kaetchen, you are right. How could I permit Satan to tempt me and then succumb to it? The Lord has done so many marvelous things for us that I cannot nor ever will be able to forget." Then I saw her lifting up her head to the sky. "Forgive me, Lord, for doubting You. I am sorry, Lord."

On the way home, we received a scary surprise. "Russians! There are Russians! They have already seen us—let's turn back to the cemetery," Mutti exclaimed, panic-stricken.

"No," Onkel Emil said, "they have definitely seen us. We have to continue walking. Try to act as though you're not afraid."

The Russians were sitting at the edge of the woods around a large fire. Suddenly Dieter took off toward their small group at top speed.

"Lord, protect him," Mutti prayed out loud.

Onkel Emil told us to pray fervently, but to keep walking. We kept an eye on Dieter and the soldiers. Before there was time to do much worrying, my brother moved away from the troops and came running back toward us.

"Look, Mutti," Marlies called out. "He is carrying something. He has something under each arm."

In no time he had caught up to us. Totally out of breath, he stuttered, "Look, Mutti! Look!"

Mutti was so touched by the sight of his treasures that she wept. Kaetchen joined her, for under one arm Dieter carried a large loaf of dark bread and under the other a whole barbequed piglet. Everyone was shocked at the sight of this miracle. Mutti ran her hand through Dieter's curly hair and cried.

We were still eating from that piglet a few days later when we had another adventure. "I smell smoke," Onkel Emil said as he returned from work and entered the kitchen.

"I don't smell anything," Mutti answered, throwing a few small chips of red cattle salt into the pot. "I think what you probably smell are our boiling piglet bones. We are having bone soup tonight. When we add your soup, Emil, to this kettle, we shall have a true feast."

"Come, Emil," Kaetchen said, pulling him by the arm, "come into the living room and rest your weary leg. We'll call you when dinner is ready."

"I smell something now, too," Mutti said a few moments later. She opened the black metal door of the stove to check on the burning sticks, and in an instant enough smoke escaped to fill the whole kitchen. Although she stoked the fire and closed the door, smoke began to filter through the cracks in the door. "Something is definitely wrong, Kaetchen."

Onkel Emil came back into the kitchen. "What is all the commotion about? Aha! Emil's nose isn't so bad after all, is it? Now the little women are having problems they can't solve, right? Why don't they let this man help them?" he asked with a big grin on his face. "Here, Liane, you hold my cane while I find the problem." He pulled the metal latch on the door to check on the fire and again thick smoke billowed into the kitchen. Most of it quickly found its way through the large open window to the courtyard. After checking the stovepipe and vents, Onkel Emil concluded that the chimney was clogged. "We are in trouble. We need a chimney sweep."

"Where can we find a chimney sweep?" Kaetchen asked, laughing. "The chimney sweep is no longer in Lippehne. He was in the army, and who knows where he might be today."

When Mutti checked our bone soup, it was no longer boiling. The sticks had turned to warm ashes.

"So what does the man propose we do?" she teased.

"We have to do the job ourselves. We have to clean the chimney."

"You certainly can't do it, Emil," Mutti declared. "How will you get through the attic window, onto the roof, and to the chimney on one leg? That's impossible."

"And Kaetchen is too small and skinny. The wind will blow her right off the roof," Onkel Emil added.

"So that leaves me," Mutti continued her joking, "an able-bodied, strong woman."

"We should wait a bit and make sure that the fire is out completely," Kaetchen said. "In the meantime I'll go to the coal shed and get Vati's chimney brush. I think he had one in there somewhere." With those words she dashed out of the kitchen and returned a few minutes later with a large metal coil and a brush.

"Emmy, be careful! Get on the step stool, now—there! When you have braced yourself we'll give you a push to help you out the window."

"Don't push too hard or I'll end up on the sidewalk, face down. This window is made for slender people only, that's for sure—oh, no, I can't climb up there!" We could only see half of Mutti as she twisted around to stare up at the chimney. "Do you have any idea how steep this roof is?"

"You are the only one who can do it, Emmy." Kaetchen encouraged her. "Just don't look down—keep your eyes on the chimney."

After Mutti was out of sight, we all listened to the steel brush scraping the walls of the chimney.

"Lippehne has a new chimney sweep: Emmy Guddat," Onkel Emil announced. "I am amazed what that woman can do."

It was to be more difficult to get Mutti back into the attic than it had been to get her out. She handed the brush in first, then slid in as best she could. When she turned around, we all began to roar. Her face was black with soot, and the whites of her eyes seemed to stand out from her face. Our laughing became so loud that the children dashed upstairs to join in.

"Well," Mutti said, trying to wipe a sooty face with sootier hands, "my mother told me that a girl has to be able to do everything, but I never thought that would include sweeping a chimney."

11
The First Attempt

"**M**y son is coming home! My son is coming home!" Kaetchen burst into the house a few days later, singing and bubbling over with joy. "The doctor said he can come home tomorrow. He has to eat well, I am told, to regain his strength. That order will present a real problem from the human point of view, but it will be no problem for our Lord. The Almighty can help, and I know He will."

Everyone was excited about Hanno's return, Dieter especially. His friend was coming home! When Kaetchen carried a little bundle of skin and bones into the house the next day, though, we realized that it would be a long time before anyone could play with Hanno. Even little Vilmar's excitement quickly vanished when he looked at his brother.

Hanno spent all his time in bed. We were allowed to visit him, but he was oblivious to our presence.

"Rejoice!" Mutti tried to encourage Kaetchen. "Look what my customer just brought me—one whole loaf of white bread. One half is for you, Kaetchen."

"Oh, thank you, Emmychen! Thank you, Lord!" With tears wetting her face, Kaetchen quickly cut a slice of the bread and took it to Hanno. He nibbled at it very slowly, finally finishing the whole slice. After a week of having one slice a day, he miraculously became stronger.

No one had molested us in weeks, and everyone gathered strength at night while the typhoid sign remained on the door. The leaves were beginning to prepare for the last splendor of another year, and soon the trees would be decked in yellows and golds. Eventually they would drop, helping to protect the earth beneath with all its dormant life. The little seedlings would be safe from the onslaught of winter, bursting forth with new life in the spring. The decaying leaves would also give them some of the nutrients they needed to become strong plants.

The days continued to grow shorter, creating an increasing problem for Onkel Emil, who had to work on sewing orders at home in the evenings. "I am going to the Polish headquarters to see if we can be hooked into the town's electrical system," Onkel Emil told us. "The days are just getting too short, and I can no longer finish orders. I will inform the magistrate that without power at home it will be very difficult for me to meet the deadlines of the Polish and Russian government."

What a wonderful surprise we had a few days later when someone turned on the light switch, and we realized that we had electrical power. It didn't really bother us too much that blackouts occurred frequently. We knew it must have been difficult for the Polish workers to familiarize themselves with the German power system.

"I will help you get to the West," Mutti's Polish friend told her one day when she picked up a dress. "If you will sell me your silverware," she continued, "I will pay you five thousand zlotys."

"Oh, no," Mutti said and looked very surprised. "That is not enough. It is real silver, and there are complete sets for twelve people and all the extra serving spoons, ladle, meat fork, and other serving pieces."

"Five thousand zlotys is what I will give you if you want to sell it," she insisted. "That is probably enough to get you to the West."

"Are you sure?"

"I think so."

"I had no choice," Mutti told Kaetchen later. "Is there a choice between real silver and freedom? Here is the money—our tickets to freedom or groceries. What will we choose?"

"We don't have a choice but to leave. Do you think that is enough money to cover our tickets to Berlin?" Kaetchen asked.

"I hope so. It's all we have. I'm so glad we succeeded in finding a safe hiding place for the silver and were able to sell it now when we most need the money."

During our devotions that night, we thanked the Lord for the money and asked His guidance for our trip. The moment the little ones were tucked in, everyone gathered in the living room again to finalize the plans and begin preparations to leave Lippehne in two days. The neighbor across the street had again assured us that trains were leaving, and since no one else had the connections she enjoyed, everyone always accepted what she said.

There was quite a bit of excitement in our house. The thought of someday leading a normal, peaceful life again charged everyone with extra energy to do all the packing and planning. Onkel Emil would carry an extra burden—in his leg. Birth certificates and other valuable papers were rolled into tiny bundles and packed neatly into a small cloth bag, custom-made to fit into the upper cavity of his prosthesis. Everyone's wedding bands were hidden there also. For some strange reason his leg had never been searched by the enemy, a fact that all the adults were counting on for our crossing of the border.

At times, the Russians had thought that Onkel Emil was reaching for a gun when he used his hand to put the artificial leg into a position that was comfortable for him. But in spite of the pain Onkel Emil had to endure in his stump, especially during a change in the weather, the prosthesis had always been a blessing to the rest of us. Many times there would not have been the opportunity for the women to hide fast enough, had it not been for Onkel Emil's slow hobbling to the door.

"I have already had a dress rehearsal with Vilmar today," Kaetchen said chuckling. "I put one layer of clothing on him and then tied some of the valuable papers to his chest. When I finished putting several more layers of clothing on him, he said, 'Mutti, Mutti. I can't put my arms down. I am too fat.' And

117

it was true—the little fellow looked like a clown. I'll really have to work on that paper problem tomorrow. I wish I had a camera to take a picture of him."

"I'll probably run into the same problem with my children, Kaetchen, but we do have to wear layers of clothing just in case we should lose our suitcases and bundles. I know that I'll really have to work on that, too."

The following day was crammed with preparations for our journey. While the children entertained themselves, Mutti, Kaetchen, and I packed.

"Schaefle," Mutti told me, "put the embroidered tablecloths and some of the other handmade bed and table linens into the suitcase. We'll at least try to get them across the border. I spent many years doing all that work for my hope chest and it would be nice to have a reminder of our home in Insterburg."

As I placed the white linen cloth with all that gorgeous blue and yellow embroidery work into the suitcase, my mind flashed back to our huge dining room in Insterburg. For special occasions this beautiful tablecloth had covered the large table. It matched the gold-rimmed china and sparkling silver perfectly. The huge walnut buffet of the dining-room suite contained several drawers filled with linens, which Mutti had done in draw work, eyelet, and embroidery before she met Vati. Huge glass doors led from the dining room to the balcony, where we loved to play and in the winter scatter seeds and crumbs for the birds. The doors were covered by floor-length lace drapes when they were closed. On the tall stand in the cove were the most beautiful plants, blooming year-round. The china cabinet was filled with crystal vases, silver dishes, and many gifts from friends. Next to the china cabinet was a large window that overlooked about one-half mile of the Hindenburgstrasse, the main street of Insterburg. It had been from this window that I waved to Adolf Hitler when his motorcade drove down the hill toward the Marktplatz. All the schools were closed the day the Fuehrer visited our city. He looked exactly the way he did in pictures, I thought to myself. Then I loved him. Now I hated him.

"Schaefle! Liane! Stop dreaming!" Mutti called to me. "Keep at your packing. We have a lot to do today. When you are finished with that project, you can get your own clothes ready for tomorrow.

I suggest you wear two pairs of socks, your boots, and two dresses, plus the outer clothing, of course."

The neighbor from across the street suddenly appeared at the house to check on us. She saw the flurry of activity and the packing and knew for certain that we planned to leave. "Well," she said, "I see that you did decide to escape."

"I wouldn't really put it that way," Mutti replied. "We have the money and plan to purchase our tickets just like everybody else. I wouldn't really call that 'escape.' "

"Well, you know what I mean. So, if I don't see you again, have a safe trip, and goodbye."

The farmer's wife who stayed at our house in January offered her help in getting us to the railroad station. She told us that we could use her haywagon and her two old horses for transportation. "Please return the team and wagon to my farm after you and your belongings are at the station."

"Of course," Mutti replied. "I will return them personally."

"You, Frau Guddat? You are such a refined lady from the city. You don't know how to handle horses, do you?"

"Of course. I was raised on a farm. My parents owned a large farm near Heydekrug, in East Prussia. I do know how to handle a team of horses and a wagon."

"That's interesting. I would never have thought that someone like you knew what it was like to have dirty hands."

When Onkel Emil returned from work, the hallway was filled with bundles and suitcases. He finished his packing in a very short time by putting all of his belongings into a duffle bag. "I am finished packing," he announced. "You ladies have packed for two days now and are still going strong? How can that be?"

"No comment," Mutti said.

Our devotional time was very sad that day. This was our last evening on the little farm! Where would we live next? Where would we be by this time tomorrow night?

"Only the Lord knows," Mutti told me.

I thought it must be especially difficult for Kaetchen to leave her parents' home. She had already given up her own home, and now she had to suffer the loss of another place dear to her. I felt rather depressed that night, too, but how much more difficult it must have been for Kaetchen.

"Lord, we commit our way to You. We know that You will lead us and direct our paths tomorrow. We love You, and we implore You to strengthen us and protect us," Onkel Emil prayed. "Guide us with Your eyes as You have done so many times in the past. Lord, save us from this system of deprivation. Unite us with our loved ones soon. Help all the children to be in good spirits tomorrow, and let everything go smoothly. We thank You for answering our prayers, and we bless Your wonderful name. Amen!"

"Let's leave the house at 6:30 A.M.," Onkel Emil suggested. "That will give us an extra hour to get to the station. It will also give Emmy sufficient time to return the horses and wagon and about half an hour or so for anything unforeseen."

"Everything sounds fine to me, Emil. Do you know what?"

"What, Kaetchen?"

"It never ceases to amaze me how precise you are in figuring out time schedules for Emmy and me. We certainly wouldn't know what we'd do without you and your pocket watch."

"Sh-sh-sh, Kaetchen! Not so loud! Do you want somebody to hear you and come and turn me in for having been smart enough to keep my pocket watch out of the enemy's hands?"

"Just make sure your leg doesn't start ticking when we have to go through inspection somewhere tomorrow," Mutti joined in the fun.

"That's enough, you ladies! I see you are getting tired and giddy. Let's make a quick check of everything and then go to bed. We have to be alert for our trip."

"Good idea!"

"The last night in our feather beds," Mutti added. "Only the Lord knows where we will sleep tomorrow."

What a gorgeous morning! It promised to be a nice day. There was not a cloud in the sky, and the little ones were as chipper as the birds. After a soup breakfast, we all left. Mutti was ready with the wagon, the luggage was loaded, and Kaetchen locked the house and put the key in her coat pocket. Mutti was softly humming the song,

Even though I don't know the way,
You surely know it, Lord,
That makes my soul quiet and peaceful.

Mutti's humming and cheerfulness calmed me, too.

We arrived at the station with plenty of time to spare. Quickly everybody helped unload the luggage so that Mutti and Dieter could return the team. While we organized the suitcases and bundles, which had just been thrown off the wagon, we noticed that we were being watched closely by some men who stood idly around the station. One of them slowly wandered past our belongings, suddenly turned, grabbed one of our bundles, and ran off. Onkel Emil tried to limp after him, shouting angrily, but the thief continued to run. From then on we were each assigned a suitcase or bundle to sit on and one to hold on to.

Slyly the men continued to move around us. "There is no train running," one of them told us, but we pretended not to hear him. We waited and waited, several hours. We had not seen any railroad personnel. Could it be true?

"I hear something," Dieter said excitedly. "I hear the tracks humming! Come over here and listen!"

My heart began to jump.

"Our freedom train!" Mutti rejoiced. "I hear it, too. Our freedom train!"

"Everybody grab some luggage, quickly!" Onkel Emil's voice grew sharp.

"I am ready!" My eyes followed the tracks into an endless stretch of meadows. "Yes, there it is! It is coming closer."

"Why isn't it slowing down, Mutti?" Dieter asked. What he said was true. The train was moving too fast. It whizzed right past us and the Lippehne station. Nobody said a word, not even when another thief took off with one of our suitcases. Onkel Emil swung his cane at him, but it was too late. He got away.

"That must not have been our train," Onkel Emil reasoned.

Utterly speechless and with our hopes dashed, we all stood in a discouraged little group, the sound of the train still ringing in our ears.

"Did we pray enough about our departure?" Mutti began to analyze our predicament. "Perhaps it was only our will to leave and not the Lord's. We were all so busy preparing for our journey that even our devotions were cut short."

"You may be right, Emmy. We have been awfully busy. Maybe our time to leave Lippehne has not yet come."

"That is all right, Mutti," Hanno said. "I like Opi's farm. It is so much better than the hospital. I like to go back to the farm."

"I think you will go back to the farm. Dieter and I will go and borrow the horses and wagon again before it gets dark. We'll see you later."

Mutti took Dieter's hand, and a few minutes later, we watched him and his "old grandmother" slowly turn the first street corner and head toward the promenade. It was safer to walk there than through the center of town.

The little ones were very hungry and restless, and so were the adults. Those men prowling around us had to be watched every single second. Apparently they had no intentions of letting us out of their sight. They knew, of course, that we had packed only our very best things. At last, Mutti was coming with the team and wagon. Quickly we loaded what we had left back on the wagon.

"The longer we stay here," Onkel Emil told me in a very disappointed tone, "the longer we all have to wait for a reunion with our loved ones."

"I am so anxious to see Vati, and so is Mutti. Why then couldn't the Lord let us get away today?"

"It must not have been His time, Liane."

"What is going on at our little farm, Kaetchen?" Dieter asked nervously, peering over the bundles on the wagon.

"What do you mean, Dieter? What do you see from up there?"

"I see people coming out of the little farm. They carry things."

"What do they carry?"

"I don't know. I can't see."

Yes, suddenly we saw it, too. People were marching in and out of our house, but by the time we arrived, the front door was wide open and not a soul was in sight anywhere. The whole street was empty. As we looked across the street, our neighbor sat knitting in her usual chair at the window.

"Lord, we thank You for this little place which You have preserved for us." Onkel Emil began praying while we were all still seated on the wagon. "We can't thank You enough for the miracle You performed again today."

I wondered how he could even pray such a prayer. We hadn't gained our freedom; the robbers took our luggage; the house had been ransacked; our hopes of seeing our loved ones were dashed; I just didn't understand. There was absolutely nothing to be thankful for as far as I was concerned.

"Yes, there is," Mutti whispered in my ear while Onkel Emil was still praying.

How did Mutti know what I was thinking?

"We did not lose our home, Schaefle. Someone could have easily moved in here while we were gone, but no one did. That is a true miracle."

12
Advent

The trees were bare; the flowers had been killed by the first frost; the air was nippy. Seldom did the sun warm the earth as the days became shorter. At times my own soul seemed to get entangled in this gloomy picture. I thought about the days at my grandparents' farm and all the delicious food we used to eat. I thought of the sugar eggs at Omi's house. I thought of the good times we had had when Vati was still with us. I reveled in those memories often, but hardly ever finished my dream without being jolted back into reality, realizing that all those things and the people that were dear to me were now part of the past. At times I found myself becoming lifeless, even though my heart was still beating within me.

On our begging trip one day, something pleasant happened to reverse that trend. We noticed people on the street with handwagons loaded with sugar beets.

"A mystery! I will solve that mystery," Dieter proclaimed. "Where did people get those beets?"

It didn't take us long to trace the beets back to a large farm outside of town.

"Dieter, can you imagine thousands of pounds of sugar beets lying in those caches undiscovered all year? They are from last year's crop. Why hasn't anyone found them sooner?" No one at home was able to answer that question for us. It must have been a special surprise the Lord had reserved just for that time.

Onkel Emil and Mutti took the handwagon and, with Dieter and me leading the way, hurried back to the farm. After arriving at the cache, we quickly dug under the soil and straw cover and pulled out the huge cone-shaped beets. Even though they had lain buried for one year, they were firm and had not lost moisture. Many of them must have weighed three or four pounds each. The wagon was filled in a very short time. We managed to get the heavy load home with Mutti and Onkel Emil pulling and Dieter and I pushing. Kaetchen, hearing us come, opened the passage door to the courtyard so that we could pull right in.

"What a blessing the Lord has bestowed on us today! We can give our children something sweet to eat," Mutti said to Kaetchen, bubbling with joy.

"Let's all pitch in and unload these beets," Onkel Emil suggested. "With everyone's help we'll have the job done in a few minutes."

We had a busy evening. We were all very tired, but the next morning Kaetchen was nowhere in sight. We knew her sons loved to sleep in, but she always rose early. Checking the courtyard, Mutti was surprised to find the handwagon missing.

"I think I have an idea where Kaetchen is," she remarked, entering the kitchen. "She must have gone to get sugar beets." Mutti was right. A short time later, we heard the handwagon pulling up to the yard door.

"I had to help provide for my sons," she said, looking like a child expecting punishment for having left the house without permission.

Making syrup or molasses from sugar beets was a project in which all but the little ones were involved. The beets' skins were creamy white and somewhat rough. Soil, embedded in the little crevices, was scrubbed out with a stiff brush and water. In assembly-line fashion, we all worked at cleaning the beets and then peeling them.

"I'll start cutting them into pieces," Mutti said. "By the time Onkel Emil comes home from work tonight, we can build a fire under the large kettle and start boiling the beet chips. Can you imagine syrup on bread? Sweet, dark, thick syrup?"

My mouth was watering at the thought. It was that vision that immediately gave all of us a fresh surge of energy to continue the boring and strenuous chore. Mutti's and Kaetchen's hands were getting blisters, and their arms were sore from cutting up the hard roots. Only with the encouraging words of hymns and telling of jokes did the job become more bearable. All day we were munching on beet chips. Our tastebuds must have been surprised to encounter something sweet—something they hadn't tasted all year.

Onkel Emil pitched in at night with the syrup project. He also set everything up for a good fire the next morning.

"I think we should all get a good night's sleep and rise early in the morning to light the fire and start the boiling process. You ladies will then have to keep the fire going all day. In the evening we take turns tending it and stirring the beets. Is everyone in agreement?"

"No objections," Mutti said.

Eventually, after the pulp had been removed, the boiling produced half a kettle full of liquid. The mixture was boiled slowly for two more days until a dark, thick syrup remained. The processing of the second load of beets was finished by the first Sunday of Advent, and prayers of thanksgiving and praise were offered with a new joy during our devotions. One of the foremost prayers continued to be for our freedom. "Lord, help us gain our freedom, but not our will, but Yours, shall be done. You can move heaven and earth to take us out of Lippehne. We don't know why You delay answering our request, but give us patience. Help us to rely continually on You for guidance. Don't let our own will get in Your way. Let us be a true witness for You, even before our enemies." This and similar prayers were offered daily.

Advent! What a time of celebration! This was the first of the four Sundays before Christmas. It was a time of preparing our hearts for the birthday of our Lord. The poems Mutti wrote for everyone, young and old, were almost committed to memory. Mutti was making an Advent wreath from the evergreen branches Dieter and I brought home.

"We don't have four candles to place into the greens of the wreath," she said apologetically. "So this year one candle will have to suffice. It has to last until Christmas—we can light it only for a short time during our celebrations."

Refuge

The first night that we lit the candle was a thought-provoking evening for me. As I watched the sparkle from the reflection of the light in everyone's eyes, I remembered what Mutti had told me. She said that our eyes had become dull because of the lack of vitamins. Now I understood what she meant. Udo looked especially cute tonight with his twinkling eyes and bleached blond hair. Marlies, with her china doll face and almost white curls, was doing what everyone else was—enjoying the slight flickering of our Advent candle. Hanno's face still looked sallow, but both his and Vilmar's eyes sparkled in the reflected candlelight. When I studied Dieter's face, I saw joy in him also, even though he had to suffer so much with his open leg sores.

"Fellowshipping with our family is just wonderful, isn't it?" Mutti said softly, as if she had read my mind. "What would we do without our big family here? What would we do without each other? The Lord is so good to us, isn't He?"

It was often difficult for me to understand how Mutti could be so thankful and joyous. I sometimes saw her saddened and weeping, but usually she was happy. How could she be so happy tonight? Had she forgotten our beautiful Emmanuel church in Insterburg and what it was like there at this special season? A huge, decorated Advent wreath, hung from the high ceiling of the church, thrilled hundreds of our church friends. Vati would open the Advent service by playing the huge pipe organ, one of the largest in all of Germany. The whole building would vibrate when he played, and the choir sang "Lo, How a Rose" and many other songs pointing to the birth of Jesus. Bible passages would be read, and praises would be offered to the Lord with Advent songs. In Sunday school we children would have the final rehearsals for the Christmas pageant.

What do we have now? Memories. Nothing but memories. That was a lot to be thankful for, Mutti reminded me. As I seriously considered that, I tended to agree.

Onkel Emil opened the Christmas season for us by reading the story of the conception of Jesus from the book of Luke in the New Testament: "He shall be great, and shall be called the Son of the Highest: and the Lord God shall give unto him the throne of his father David: And he shall reign over the house of Jacob for ever; and of his kingdom there shall be no end." He read most of that first chapter and then prayed.

"Why do we have to blow out the candle before we sing, Mutti?" Dieter asked. "Can't we do it after our songs?"

"No, my son, we have to do it now. We have to be able to light it for three more Sundays, and if we use it all up now, we will have nothing left."

The last look I saw on everyone's face before Vilmar blew out the candle was a sad one. During the singing of our beautiful Advent songs, however, I sensed that all the faces in the room must have been smiling again. No one could sing so joyously with a grumpy face.

In the following weeks, Onkel Emil received many requests to sew. His reputation was growing among the Polish people, but he had little extra time to do more work. He and all of his assistants worked on army uniforms six days a week. In the evenings he was tired and worn out. His payment remained the same: watery soup and one slice of bread. His co-workers often shared heartbreaking stories with one another, and often Onkel Emil returned home totally depressed. Most of the stories were of struggles to survive and hopes for escape.

Dieter and I had become professional scavengers by this time, but the Lord still continued to provide for us in unexpected ways. One day we returned home just in time to hear Kaetchen saying goodbye to a Polish visitor. "Goodbye, and thank you again," she said as she closed the front door. "Emmychen, you can't imagine what my friend just gave me! One bar of soap—soap! What luxury! I had to laugh when she lifted up her skirt and pulled the soap out of her bloomers. She was laughing, too. I guess not even the vilest system can keep people from helping one another. Isn't that marvelous?"

Sometimes Dieter and I were sent hunting for things other than food or firewood—like a Christmas tree. That one was a tough assignment.

"We have to walk faster, Dieter. My arm is getting numb."

"I can't walk faster. We should have cut a smaller tree. I never knew Christmas trees were so heavy."

"Don't complain. I think it will be worth it when we see it all decorated with the paper chains we made and the Scheeren-schnitt snowflakes."

"Why don't we stop right here on the street and shorten the tree? Then it won't be so heavy."

"No, we can't do that! We have to drag it home like this."

Mutti and Kaetchen were delighted when they saw us pulling such a beautiful tree into the house. They immediately confiscated it and told us that we would not be able to see it again until we celebrated the birth of our Lord the next day.

"If we can't help with the tree, we should go and finish memorizing the Christmas story, Liane."

Upstairs in our room, Dieter and I settled down on the couch for some serious mental exercise.

"Let's continue, Liane!" Dieter commanded, and his dark eyes looked stern. "We have to finish memorizing the Christmas story. Only three more verses to go."

" 'And they that heard it wondered at those things which were told them by the shepherds. But Mary kept all these things and pondered them in her heart. But the shepherds returned. . . .' Sure wish I could have been one of the first people on earth to see the baby Jesus," Dieter interrupted us. " 'Glorifying and praising God for all the things that they had heard and seen, as it was told unto them. . . . ' "

"Do you smell something baking, Liane?"

"That can't be." We held our noses in the air like rabbits that have detected the scent of fresh lettuce in someone's garden. It was true. Something was baking. It was no use, though, to continue guessing what it might be. We were simply not allowed to go into the kitchen without permission on this day before Christmas Eve, and not even Dieter was able to solve the mystery of the delicious aroma that was trailing upstairs.

Christmas Eve morning! What an exciting day this was going to be! As I looked out the window, I realized that the earth was lightly dusted with snow, our first snow. The wind took the little flakes and pushed them into little swirls that danced around on the sidewalk. Airy snow clouds were being swept off the schoolhouse roof. They were joining the flakes below. A short, old lady with a black babushka and long, black skirt was shuffling along the school building. She was weighted down by a bundle of firewood. Her long skirt swept a bare path on the sidewalk, which the little flakes covered again quickly. She looked lifeless and uncaring. I wondered if she would be celebrating Christmas tonight.

The afternoon seemed long. The sky was dark, and the clouds released a few snow flurries every now and then. Why did I have to take a nap today along with the little ones? I knew they had to be wide awake for our celebration tonight, but I could have managed without a nap. Even though this had been the rule at our house ever since I could remember, I really thought an exception could be made for someone my age. Taking a nap on Christmas Eve afternoon was nothing but torture. I knew it freed Mutti to decorate the tree without interruption and wrap the gifts, but what I couldn't understand was why all those activities took such an awfully long time.

The bread soup seemed to taste extra good that night. It must have been the beet syrup sweetening that made it so special.

"Yes, Pittimaus," Mutti was trying to answer some of Marlies's chattering questions. "We will all put on our Sunday clothes. You wouldn't go to a birthday party unless you were dressed up, right? And tonight we are celebrating the birthday of Jesus. Even though we can't see Him, we dress up for His special day."

It was almost dark when we all filed into the living room. The beautiful tree stood in the corner, one candle perched near the top of the branches. Everyone was singing: "O come, little children, O come one and all, O come to the cradle in Bethlehem's stall." The singing continued after we had found our favorite seats in the living room. "O Tannenbaum," "Softly Falleth the Snow," "O Thou Glorious," and many other traditional German Christmas songs made this celebration more special than any other we'd had in the course of the year.

Hanno and Vilmar were radiant with joy as they quoted Isaiah 9:6: "For unto us a child is born, unto us a son is given: and the government shall be upon his shoulder: and his name shall be called Wonderful, Counsellor, The mighty God, The everlasting Father, The Prince of Peace."

Those two little ones were very deserving of the applause they received.

It was almost pitch-dark outside, and I couldn't wait for that one candle to be lit. A few more songs, songs the German people have enjoyed for hundreds of years, warmed our hearts. Finally Onkel Emil got up and very deliberately limped toward the tree. Striking a wooden match, he lit the candle. He hobbled back

131

to his chair and with both hands lifted his prosthesis into a position that was comfortable for him.

When I looked around the room, I saw sixteen eyes focused on that one candle. No one said a word. Everyone just enjoyed the candle's warm glow and the brightness it gave all of us. Suddenly Mutti broke the long silence:

"The light of the world is Jesus. Today is Jesus' birthday. Let's hear the birthday story, Schaefle and Dieter."

Standing next to the tree, we gave a curtsy and a bow and began reciting Luke 2:1-20: "And it came to pass in those days, that there went out a decree from Caesar Augustus, that all the world should be taxed . . . ."

Our performance was flawless and our audience attentive. Were Mutti's eyes filled with tears? Udo sat patiently on her lap, and she gave him a few extra squeezes.

"We will all pray now," Onkel Emil continued, "and thank God for giving us His only Son on this Christmas Day."

"I know that verse, Onkel Emil," Marlies interrupted. Sliding off the couch and placing herself in front of the Christmas tree, she curtsied and said: "For God so loved the world, that he gave his only begotten Son, that whosoever believeth in him should not perish, but have everlasting life." A quick curtsy, and she jumped back onto the couch with a big smile, her natural curls dancing around her head.

"That is wonderful, Pittimaus! You quoted that verse well!"

"God gave all of us a gift, a present, on this special day many, many years ago," Onkel Emil continued. "He gave it to the whole world, to every single person. And this gift is Jesus. You children all know the story of Adam and Eve, don't you? And you know that they did wrong. They sinned. Because of them we are all sinners, too. God loves people so much and wants to fellowship with them, but the people always want to go their own way. Then God told the people to offer sacrifices and confess their sins. Many animals had to die."

"Is that when little lambs had to die?" Dieter asked.

"Yes, Dieter, that is right. Innocent lambs. But one day God said: 'That is enough. I will send my own Son to earth, and He will be the last sacrifice ever. He will die on the cross. He will be buried, and I will raise Him from the dead and take Him back to heaven to live with me. I will give everyone on earth a choice. They can believe on my Son, thank Him for dying for them, and come to live with us in heaven for eternity, or they can reject my gift and forever burn in hell.' So, you see, God really loves us a lot, doesn't He? He gives us the very best gift He has—His Son. Many people don't want to accept God's gift. They don't want to ask Jesus into their hearts. But I hope you will not reject Him. Your mommies and I have asked for forgiveness of our sins many years ago and asked Jesus to come into our lives, and He did. We talk to Him every day in prayer, and we read the road map to heaven, the Bible. Jesus gives us peace and joy. He gives us strength, and we are looking forward to spending eternity with Him. Do you know what eternity means?"

"Yes," Hanno answered. "It means forever, and ever, and ever, and ever, and ever, and ever. . . ."

"That's enough, Hanno," Vilmar broke in.

"You children know how good the Lord has been to us during these difficult days," Onkel Emil continued. "He has protected us. He has shown us so many miracles. He helps us to survive even though we don't have much to eat. He keeps our minds strong, and He will bring all of our families together again."

"But why didn't God protect Opi from typhoid?" Hanno asked. "Why did he have to die?"

"That is a good question, Hanno, but I don't have the answer to it. I can, however, imagine that Jesus said to Himself: 'That Opi Lehmann is very special to me. He has loved me ever since I became his Saviour. He has lived for me. He has told many other people about me. He is very special. I think I want him to come and live in heaven with Me.' And then Jesus took him to heaven to live there forever and ever."

Kaetchen's eyes were filled with tears. "Emil, you said that so beautifully. Thank you!"

Our festivities continued with the singing of "Stille Nacht" and praying. The homecoming poems were recited, and we sang more songs. Mutti herself recited a poem, dealing with the Germans being to blame for all the trouble in which Germany found itself because they rejected the grace of God.

Our candle was rather short now, but continued to shed its glow on those who, with great fascination, sat and admired it.

"Children," Mutti announced. "God gave us two gifts tonight. One is the gift of His Son and another one is under the tree. We'll let Udo go and get the gift that is for everyone."

Udo slipped off Mutti's lap and reached for whatever was under the large doily. When the doily fell off, we couldn't believe our eyes. It was a plate full of cookies. Cries of excitement and surprise came from almost everyone.

"Cookies! Cookies! Cookies!"

"There are two millet cookies for each man, woman, and child," Mutti announced joyfully. "How is that for a Christmas surprise?"

"Two cookies?" Hanno exclaimed. "What a feast!"

"I will save one of my cookies for tomorrow," Marlies declared. "Tomorrow is Christmas Day, Mutti, right?"

"Yes, it is, Pittimaus."

"Emmychen, I just can't praise the Lord enough for His goodness to us," Kaetchen rejoiced. "On this Christmas Day, my Polish friend came to pay us a visit. When she saw our Christmas tree, she said: 'You German people do what we Polish folks would never dare do.'

" 'What is that?' I asked her, and she said 'We would never dare put up a Christmas tree.' Then she lifted up her skirt, and guess what she had under it to give us on this special day?"

"Why don't you tell me?"

"Under her skirt she carried a can of goat's milk as a Christmas gift for us. Can you believe the goodness of our Lord? A gift, straight from heaven, for our children."

"That is a true miracle, Kaetchen. I just hope that when we are able to serve our children full glasses of milk every day, we will not forget the miracle the Lord performed today."

"You said that beautifully, Emmychen, and I agree. In the good days we usually tend to forget how the Lord has shown Himself faithful to us in times of trouble."

13
Capture

January 1, 1946! Would this be the year the Lord would reunite our families? Would this be the year we could leave Lippehne? While we had these and many other questions on our minds, rumors were starting that more Germans would have to leave town.

"We will not be able to go because of my job," Onkel Emil said. "They would never let me go, I was told. But we know that with God all things are possible. We can't stay here. In order to be reunited with our families, we have to leave. We must pray hard and seek God's guidance. People tell me that trains leave for Berlin daily now. This fact can be to our advantage. Two women from my tailor shop have been whispering about visiting Berlin and beginning the search for their loved ones."

Mutti's eyes lit up when Onkel Emil shared that information.

"I have relatives in Berlin," she said. "Perhaps my aunt and her husband have heard where Emil is."

"But, Mutti, you can't leave!" I objected. "You can't leave us here alone."

"You won't be alone, Liane. Onkel Emil and I would be here to help you, should your Mutti decide to go," Kaetchen intervened.

"But if something happens to Mutti, who will take care of the four of us?"

"Schaefle, we belong to the Lord. He will take care of us—but I don't even know yet if I am going. I really have to pray much about this and seek the Lord's guidance."

The next day Onkel Emil returned home with more details about the trip the ladies had planned.

"The ladies have worked ahead feverishly, so that I would give them six days off. Not two but four ladies are taking the trip, Emmy. The neighbor from across the street is one of them. She is going along as their interpreter. The women told me that anyone is welcome to join them. Since the war has been over for months now, they don't foresee any problems."

"Did you find out, Emil, when they plan to leave?"

"Yes. They expect to leave on January 10 and return on January 16."

"Oh, good," Mutti said, took a deep breath, and hugged me. "If I go, I'll be home on your birthday, Schaefle. I wouldn't want to miss the birthday of my oldest child."

I couldn't bear the thought of Mutti's leaving. Even though everyone was still praying about it, I had the feeling that she would go to Berlin. I knew it had been very difficult for her without Vati, and if she could learn where he was, life would be easier for her. I determined to help even more with my brothers and sister to make Mutti's dream come true.

"If I go to Berlin, Schaefle, you will be in charge of everyone during the day while Onkel Emil is at work. Kaetchen, of course, will assist you in any way she can. You have helped me so much with your brothers and sister that I know you can handle things beautifully. With the Lord giving you strength, you won't fail. Tell me now, honestly, how do you feel about my going?"

"I wish you wouldn't have to leave, Mutti, but if you can locate Vati, I'll be very happy. So I am all set to take over for you."

"Thank you, Schaefle! Thank you!"

As January 10 approached, I felt less strong, but couldn't let Mutti detect that. She had made the decision to go, and her rucksack was packed. Our time of devotions was sad for me. I would miss Mutti so much. I was glad it was dark in the room so that I could hide my tears.

Prayers and goodbyes were said hurriedly the next morning. The neighbor from across the street would walk to the station with Mutti and meet the others there. We were not to accompany her.

"I love you, children. The Lord keep you." These words lingered in the cold winter air as Mutti stepped into the street.

When I turned around, Kaetchen was right there to embrace me. I needed her comforting hug.

"I have always wanted a daughter like you," she told me, "but instead of giving me a daughter, the Lord has blessed me with three wonderful sons. The oldest one, of course, is in heaven now. Is it all right with you if I consider you my daughter for the next six days?"

"That would be just wonderful, Kaetchen. I think you know how much I love you."

"Now, Liane, if you need anything, I'll be right here to help you in any way I can," she added, giving me another hug. Kaetchen's offer thrilled me, but I still sensed a huge burden of responsibility.

My brothers and sister were wonderful. They were obedient and helpful to me in many little ways. When Udo needed help dressing, Marlies helped him. When Marlies required help, Dieter assisted her. Dieter was also my right hand because he could entertain everyone so well. Playing mailman and post office was one of the favorite games then. Hanno and Vilmar always joined in the fun.

One day Dieter and I walked to the bakery to buy bread. The bread line shrank very slowly, but after two hours of standing in the cold, we were getting excited about reaching the warm store. There were only ten more people ahead of us. Suddenly Polish words, which we had learned to recognize, were passed to the end of the queue: "No more bread today."

Very disappointed and hungry we trudged home. On the way we decided that we would leave at 7:00 A.M. tomorrow. Surely no one would be there that early and we would be first in line. When we arrived, however, quite a few women were already lined up past the store and several houses. As we waited, we constantly stomped our feet to keep them from freezing. Everyone else was doing the same, but nobody managed to stay warm today. It was just too frigid. Our bodies were numb from the

137

cold. The wait was worthwhile that day, for two hours later we returned home with a loaf of dark bread. I spent the rest of the day cleaning and scrubbing Onkel Emil's room and the staircase. Tomorrow was Mutti's homecoming day.

Finally, it was January 16: my birthday and Mutti's homecoming! Kaetchen and Onkel Emil sang a choir number for me.

"With this song we wish you the Lord's richest blessing for the coming year. May our Lord give you health and joy, and may He return your Vati to you and your family. May the Lord keep you and watch over you," Kaetchen said as she cupped both of my hands in hers. She then gave me a hug and a kiss.

"Kaetchen's wishes are mine, too, Liane. The Lord bless you." Onkel Emil, who was about six feet and two inches tall, bent down to give me a kiss. As I was standing there in the kitchen, a line of five little well-wishers filed past. What a way to start my birthday! I was so touched by all the fuss everybody made because I was twelve years old.

While Dieter and the children entertained themselves, I started my workday by making the beds.

"I want to help, Liane," Marlies said as she suddenly appeared to assist in straightening out the feather bed. I had fluffed the feathers almost perfectly, but what were her little hands doing to it? The bed resembled a camel after she left, and I had to start "building the bed" all over again. In typical German fashion, I worked and worked on the beds to give them a smooth, square look. The feathers had to be pushed in just the right direction to achieve that. After that job was done, I continued to work toward my goal: to have all the darning and mending done by the time Mutti returned. While I sat near the window and darned, I heard Onkel Emil's voice downstairs. What was he doing at home at noon? He had never come home at this time of day.

"Liane! Dieter!" his deep voice rolled upstairs. "Come on down, you two!" In seconds Dieter and I were reporting to him. "Let's go into the living room. I have to tell you something. You come too, Kaetchen," he said as we passed through the kitchen. "Let's all sit down."

When we were seated he continued, "I heard some disturbing news today. I heard that all the Germans who returned from Berlin by train yesterday were arrested by Russian soldiers and taken to jail. It is probable that this will happen again today. Those who were seized were walking out of the main gate of the station. Others had no problems. We cannot allow them to capture your mother. So I suggest the following safety measures: you, Liane and Dieter, go to the station to meet Mutti. Be there before the train arrives at 3:30 P.M. The moment it stops and you see your mother getting off, dash toward her—there'll be no time for hugs and kisses—and tell her to follow you quickly around the outside of the station building. You can't run. That is too conspicuous. You must walk very fast to avoid the crowd that will be filing out through the main gate. When you are away from the station, take one of the side streets home. Don't walk on Main Street! Do you understand everything? Do you know your assignment?"

"Yes, Onkel Emil," Dieter answered, "we understand."

"I think we should all pray right now about the situation," Kaetchen suggested. "We have a powerful God. He can let everything go well this afternoon."

After we had prayed for protection for Mutti and the other women, Onkel Emil left for his shop.

"If I hadn't had a sewing deadline to meet and could walk faster, I'd go to the station myself," he said. "But I know you two can do a better job warning Mutti than I can. So I'll see you all tonight."

My heart seemed to be skipping beats. We didn't have to wait until Mutti reached home? We could see her twenty minutes earlier? That was a lovely birthday surprise. I had missed her terribly. I wondered what news she had of Vati. Where was he living? Had she perhaps seen him? How was her visit with her aunt and uncle in Berlin? All these questions raced through my mind. Darning was no chore today because of the joy that lay ahead. Even Onkel Emil's large sock holes were woven shut in no time. I was so glad I could keep busy until it was time to leave. A quick check showed me that Udo's face and hands had to be washed again. His blond, straight hair had to be combed even though I knew it would not stay that way until we returned from the station. Marlies's dress was neat and her curls beautiful for Mutti's homecoming. A further check showed that no one had pushed a little hand into the feather beds. The wash bowl was scrubbed and filled with clean water. Everything was just the way Mutti would like it.

After Kaetchen had prayed with us, Dieter and I bundled up and headed for the railroad station. It was a bitterly cold, snowy day. There was almost no one on the street.

"We don't have to walk so fast, Dieter. We have plenty of time."

"Aren't you anxious to see Mutti?"

"Of course. But getting there early doesn't make the train come any sooner."

"Well, yes, I know that. I just can't wait to see her."

"I know. I know, little brother. I feel the same way you do."

We walked silently for a while. I heard only the squeaking of my boots as the snow crunched beneath them. Last year, just before the Russian invasion, I had celebrated my eleventh birthday without Vati, too. On my tenth birthday Vati had called. That was also the day the Lyceum in Insterburg, the school I was to attend after elementary school, was engulfed in flames and partially destroyed. It was a terrible sight from our living room window. The most wonderful birthday memories, though, were those of our family celebrations. Opi, Omi, and Vati's twin brother would come to our house in the afternoon, eat yeast cakes and torten with us, and bring exciting gifts. A special birthday or winter treat was always apples baked in the tile oven. Why did my thoughts always stray to food? It wasn't fair to my body. The saliva glands experienced too many disappointments.

Just a few more steps past the rotting furniture, the pianos, and the sewing machines, and we would turn to go around the depot to wait there.

"If we stay right here at the corner of the building," Dieter whispered, "we can see the train coming and overlook all the cars at the same time."

"Good thinking, Brother! Good idea!"

The tracks were beginning to hum, and we knew that we would see Mutti in a few moments. The train grew larger and larger as it approached Lippehne. The whistle gave off a deafening sound as the brakes squeaked and caused the mass of metal to come to a screeching halt. The conductor stuck his head out of the window of the engine compartment and called, "Lippehne!"

My heart was racing.

"There she is! Come, Liane! Mutti! Mutti!" Was it really Mutti? She looked so tired. Her clothes were dirty, torn, and wet.

"Come quickly this way!" I said grabbing her by the arm. "They are arresting people. Don't go through the building!" We walked as fast as we could without running. Suddenly two Russians ran toward us with their rifles aimed at us.

"You come! You come!" they yelled and yanked Mutti by the arm.

"But I have children!"

"You come!"

"I want to say goodbye to my children." She tried to turn around to see us, but they pushed her ahead of them.

"Mutti! Mutti!" Dieter cried. One of the Russians turned around and almost hit him with his rifle.

"Daway! Daway!" they hollered and continued to try to chase us away, but we followed. Mutti made another attempt to talk to us. As she turned around, her captors became furious and pushed her ahead of them with their rifles in her back.

"We have to follow to see where they take Mutti," I told Dieter. Sobbing, he nodded his head.

"Daway! Daway!" the Russians yelled at us again when they heard us talking. One of them turned and flung his arms angrily, motioning for us to go away. That really scared me. We walked more slowly to increase the distance between them and us. Suddenly they turned left on the street which led to the KGB headquarters.

"We can't lose them, Dieter. Let's run!" Quickly we caught up to them. The Russians noticed that immediately, and one of them started chasing after us. We had no choice now. They would kill us if we persisted. We must run home.

Kaetchen and all the children were standing in the hallway saying: "Willkommen!" as we knocked and the door opened. They naturally expected Mutti to walk in with us. Instead Dieter and I just stood on the step and cried.

"Mutti was arrested by the Russians. She was taken to headquarters." Intermingled with sobs, we told Kaetchen the whole story. The sad news caused her visible pain.

"Come into the kitchen and get warm," she told us, embracing Dieter and me.

Marlies could hardly be comforted. "I want to see Mutti. I want to see Mutti," she begged.

Udo joined the heartbreaking cries. I needed to pull myself together. It was my job now to cheer them up. I decided to play games with everybody. Onkel Emil, I felt certain, would know how to get Mutti released from jail.

14
Nothing but Trust

As we recounted the capture episode for Onkel Emil, a depressing and helpless feeling settled into my soul.

"I will use my connections and my reputation as head worker for the communist regime to get Mutti out of jail. You two bundle up, and we will all go to headquarters. They'll release Mutti tonight yet, you'll see."

We trudged through the empty streets in utter silence. In order to avoid inhaling the icy winter air, we covered our mouths with our mittened hands.

"Lord, I have only one birthday wish," I silently prayed. "Please let Mutti come home."

Onkel Emil pushed the few strands of hair, which the wind had blown down, to the back of his head. He knocked on the door of the massive stone building, the headquarters of the Russian KGB. No one answered. He pushed the large handle, but the door was locked. Most of the rooms in the building were lit except for the basement windows. Mutti wouldn't be in a dark basement! Several other structures were fenced in and the gates locked.

"Hello! Hello!" Onkel Emil called into the darkness, but there was no response.

"We could throw a snowball at one of the windows. No, I think we are better off not doing that. It seems we can't accomplish anything here tonight, children. If Mutti doesn't return tonight, we'll come back tomorrow morning."

The walk home in the bitter cold air seemed unbelievably long. The neighbor's house across the street was still dark. She must not be home yet either.

The throne of God was bombarded that night with petitions for Mutti's release.

"Lord, You know that these children need their mother," Onkel Emil prayed. "Protect her tonight. Let no harm come to her. Lord, You are testing us. May we not fail You, but may we remain faithful and true. Let us take everything as from Your hand. And please, keep up Emmy's spirit; with Your Spirit, lift up hers."

By the time we were all tucked into our beds, Mutti still wasn't home. Was she sleeping in a bed tonight? Was she warm? Was she all alone? All through the night I awakened and listened in vain for her.

Each of us had one slice of bread spread thinly with beet syrup for breakfast. I cut Udo's slice in small, bite-size pieces the way Mutti always did it. This helped him to eat the sticky substance without getting too messy. Onkel Emil planned to stop at the KGB headquarters that morning and ask for Mutti's release.

"Children, be all ready for her homecoming today. You had the house clean and in beautiful order yesterday. Do it again today."

"We will, Onkel Emil," Dieter agreed quickly. "We'll be ready."

By late afternoon, there was still no sign of Mutti.

"Mutti! Mutti! Come see this!" Hanno called to Kaetchen. "Didn't our neighbor go to Berlin with Dieter's Mutti? She is sitting in front of her window." Running to Kaetchen's bedroom window, I too saw her sitting and knitting in her favorite chair.

"Liane, you and Dieter go across the street, please, and ask our neighbor to come over for a visit," Kaetchen requested quietly and quickly.

A few minutes later, the neighbor and the two of us, along with Kaetchen, were sitting in the living room.

"Please tell us," Kaetchen opened the conversation, "what happened to all the others in the group who went to Berlin."

144

"Well, we were all arrested at the railroad station and taken into headquarters for questioning."

"Where are all the other women?"

"They are still there, I presume, if Frau Guddat isn't home yet, and I gather from your questions that she has not yet returned."

"Why do you think you were arrested?"

"Well, the Russians told me that I was a spy. Everyone going to Berlin is considered a spy. Of course I told them that this was not the case with me, and they let me go. I am glad I didn't have to stand at attention outdoors any longer. I could not have taken it. An hour was enough for me. The others were still standing under guard and shivering when I left." Throwing back her shoulders and blinking her eyes several times, she was definitely trying to impress us. Her attitude seemed more haughty than saddened by the plight of the others.

"I am glad you could get home quickly," Kaetchen said. "But did you make any attempt to help your friends?"

"Well, Frau Mecklenburg, I think I did what I could. The Russians were very friendly when I addressed them in their own language. They seem to like it when a German speaks Russian. They told me I could go home. If I would have turned around then and asked for the release of the other four women, they might have reconsidered and called me a spy, too. So when they told me to go home, I did not want to risk losing my freedom. I just left. And that is all I can tell you. I hope I have explained everything to you. I must really go now. My sauerkraut and pork is probably burned by now. Auf Wiedersehen!"

"Auf Wiedersehen!" Kaetchen said. "Thank you for coming over."

All of a sudden I felt something welling up inside me, and I realized that I despised this lady, who not too long ago taught me several new knitting techniques. My heart became faint when I thought about Mutti having to stand in the cold for hours. Her feet and hands were always sensitive to cold.

"That conversation didn't help us, Liane, did it?" Kaetchen asked after she had locked the front door. "We must pray continually for Mutti. The Lord can perform miracles today as He did in Bible times. Do you remember the story of Peter in the book of Acts? Peter was in prison. He was chained between two soldiers, and guards were stationed at the prison door. Then an angel came, loosed the chains, and told Peter to get dressed. With the Lord's messenger leading, Peter walked through the locked iron gate into the city."

"Yes, I know that story."

"You see, Liane, Mutti is in prison, and our God is the same yesterday, today, and forever. He doesn't change. What He did then, He can do today. And that is what we will pray for: a miracle that will return Mutti to us quickly."

"I have tried everything possible to get Emmy's release," Onkel Emil explained after returning home and handing Kaetchen his cabbage soup and slice of bread. "When I petitioned the Russians, they just snickered and told me to get out." Onkel Emil blew on his hands in a effort to warm them up before taking off his coat. His face was red from the cold and even his gray hair and bushy eyebrows looked frozen. "Someone said the temperature is five degrees Fahrenheit today. It would not surprise me, Kaetchen, if I just handed you frozen soup."

"That is all right, Emil. Thanks to the good Lord, we still have a fire that can warm it up," said Kaetchen as she poured the watery soup into the pot and added more water to it.

"We have to pray for a miracle," Onkel Emil said. "Only a miracle can bring Emmy back soon."

"Funny that you would put it that way. Liane and I have just come to the same conclusion," Kaetchen added.

During our devotional time we entreated the Lord to strengthen Mutti and keep her safe. We also asked for a miracle.

"I suggest you and Dieter go to the commander's headquarters again tomorrow," Onkel Emil said before we went to bed. "You don't have to hide your tears. Don't be afraid to cry. Try to get into the building, and tell the Russians you need your mother. Seeing you children plead for your mother may carry more weight with them than my going. I, of course, plan to go to intercede for her also. I'll go later in the day."

The next day I bundled up Marlies while Dieter got ready by himself, and the three of us ventured out into the deadly cold to beg for Mutti's freedom. When we arrived at the jail, two Russians chased us away from the main door.

Marlies cried bitterly, "Mutti! Mutti! Mutti, come home!" But no one seemed to hear her.

We placed ourselves under various windows and called for Mutti, yet not a single person came to the window. The two guards had been patient with us, pretending that we did not exist. Suddenly, however, one of them ran toward us. He yelled and motioned for us to leave.

"We'll stay. Don't move!" I told Dieter and Marlies. That infuriated him. He took the rifle off his shoulder, and I immediately sensed danger. "Let's run!" I commanded, and we started running home. Marlies's little feet could hardly keep up with us. She ran and sobbed as we tried to drag her along.

Onkel Emil gave a similar report in the evening: unsuccessful. Our prayers for a miracle, however, continued.

"We'll use the same tactics again today," Onkel Emil told us the next day. "You children go to the prison and cry for your mother. I will make another attempt to see the commander. Why should they want to hold these women so long? The two workers from my tailor shop must still be there also. I have had no message from them."

By evening it was plain that we had accomplished nothing. As we compared notes, we found that we all had again received the same treatment from the Russians. We were first ignored, and then we were chased away. There was not one ray of hope.

"Tomorrow we'll walk to headquarters together, and I will try another angle," Onkel Emil informed us. "I plan to tell the Russians, hopefully the commander himself, that I, as tailor, will no longer oversee the work in the shop for him. I will tell him that I refuse to head up the work crew if Emmy is not released immediately. Perhaps that will give him something to think about."

Our plans were carried out on a cold and dreary Sunday afternoon. Would this be our miracle day? Onkel Emil even gained admission into the headquarters building along with the four of us.

"You Emil Schmidtke? You see commander? Commander out of town. You back tomorrow. Commander here then."

Apparently the pressure was accomplishing something because Onkel Emil's name had filtered down to even the guards. Heavy-hearted, but clinging to a new spark of hope, we slowly walked home. I knew Udo would love to stop to make some snowballs, but we had to obey Onkel Emil, and he had told us to go straight home.

Most of the houses on our street were occupied again. Instead of curtains, there were sheets, rags, and paper covering the windows of most of the homes. This led me to believe that the new residents must be poor. The Polish folks we met on the street were all elderly. Thus far we had not seen any young people or children.

On the wings of the eagle we are carried
Across the turbulent ocean of time.

was the song Onkel Emil and I sang for Kaetchen's birthday. We had no birthday cake or gift to give her, but with our hugs and kisses we gave her all our love. It was Monday, January 21.

"Kaetchen's birth was quite a miracle," Onkel Emil stated. "What would we do without her? Where would we all be without her? It is because of her and the Lord that we are here at her dad's house. We might not have had a place to live without Kaetchen. My birthday wish and prayer for you is that you will be reunited with your husband this year."

"Mine too," I chimed in.

"We'll celebrate more tonight," he continued, as he put on his coat, ready to leave. "And don't forget to pray for a miracle today!" The hallway echoed his voice back to us.

"Thank you, Emil, thank you for the wonderful birthday wishes and the song. You are all so dear to me. And, Lord, for today I have only one request: Please set Emmy free. Please return the mother to these children. They need her. Please make this a miracle birthday, Lord."

Again Dieter and I set our rooms in order, and everything was immaculate for Mutti's homecoming. Since any day could be our miracle day, we always had to be expectant. Kaetchen watched Udo while the three of us went to the jail again. Dressed in her white fur hat and cute coat that Mutti had made, Marlies looked like a doll. She was the one who cried the loudest when we attempted to make our presence known. If only we could get a glimpse of Mutti! Then we would at least know that she was all right, I thought. Unfortunately we didn't see anyone but the guards. The snow glistened beautifully on the lake behind the headquarters building. Chunks of ice were scattered around in various areas. Ice fishermen must have chopped the holes.

"I want to go home; my feet are frozen," my little sister complained. "Please, let's go home."

148

"I am frozen, too," Dieter added.

"But we can't go home. We have to see the commander. Let's see if we can walk right past the guards into the building. We'll all hold hands and walk real fast."

"Mutti! Mutti!" Marlies called when we approached the huge door, but that was as far as we got. The Russians seemed to know what we had in mind and planted themselves, with their legs spread, between the door posts.

"Daway, daway!" they hollered at us and almost pushed us down the steps backwards. "Daway!"

We had no choice now. We had to leave again—quickly. One of the guards chased us to make sure we left. When we no longer heard the snow squeak under his heavy boots, we knew that we were not being pursued and stopped to catch our breath.

Kaetchen tried to comfort us as she did every day, but the longer Mutti was absent the more fruitless Kaetchen's efforts became.

"Come and warm your hands and feet here at the fire. Hanno! Vilmar! You boys come here, too. We have to have a prayer meeting. I feel we should pray right now for your Mutti's release. You come and sit next to Kaetchen, Udo."

"O, Lord," she began. "You see our disappointed and humble little group here. Please answer our prayers. You have performed many wonderful things in the past. You have guided us, helped us, and protected us many times. Please, give Emmy the strength to withstand everything that is put in her way today. Don't let the spirit within her weaken. Give her the assurance that her children are safe in Your care. Give her an extra measure of faith to endure all the testing. Just place Your loving arms around her and comfort her. Let her experience Your love for her in a mighty way. Keep discouragements from all of us. Forgive us for our shortcomings. We love You and in Your strength want to live for You daily. We thank You for answering our prayers. Blessed be Your Holy Name. Amen."

15
Miracle for Mutti

Because we were not able to get warm, Dieter, Marlies, and I huddled near the stove for a long time. My little sister's feet still felt like chunks of ice. I just hoped her feet hadn't been frost-damaged during the latest attempt to free Mutti. The white ring on her cheeks was finally fading, and she no longer complained about her face hurting.

"Someone is knocking on the front door," Dieter said. We all sat in shock and began to listen. The knocking grew louder, but nobody moved. What should we do? Hide? Jump into the trap basement? Then the knocking turned into banging. We knew we had to open the door, but fear kept us from moving.

"Let's all go," Kaetchen said in a weak voice. The pounding became fierce, and we all tiptoed into the hallway. "Who is it?" Kaetchen asked bravely. There was no answer. The banging continued. We stood in silence and the house vibrated from the pounding. "Who is it?" she called again.

"It's Mutti!" Dieter said. "I know it."

"How do you know?"

"We just prayed for her, didn't we?"

Reaching for the latch, Kaetchen cautiously pulled back the heavy door.

"Mutti! Mutti! Emmy! Tante Emmy! Mutti!" We were all shouting at once. "A miracle! We just prayed for you." Everybody reached out to hug Mutti and welcome her, but she quickly intervened.

"I am sorry, please stay back. Please don't touch me. I am infested with lice. I must get rid of these pests first. Then I will hug and kiss all of you," she said with tear-filled eyes. Mutti looked so drawn and haggard. Even her wide cheekbones seemed to be sunken.

"Mutti! Mutti!" Udo cried.

"I'll hug you in a little while, my son. You all go and play, and I will be done with the clean-up in no time."

A short time later, we saw Mutti's fur-lined coat lying on a pile of snow in the courtyard.

"Hopefully the cold will kill the lice," Kaetchen said.

I couldn't believe Mutti was home. Even though we had prayed earnestly for her return, I couldn't comprehend it. A quick check upstairs showed me that everything was still clean and in order. I thought Mutti would be pleased.

Once Mutti considered herself presentable and safe, there was no end to all the embracing, loving, and kissing. Udo and Marlies clung to Mutti like burdock to a piece of clothing.

"Children, our God is wonderful. Do you know that I am the only one who was released from prison, the only one of more than twenty people? That is a real miracle of God—except our neighbor, of course, was set free immediately."

"Emmy! Emmy! Thank God you are back!" Onkel Emil walked in to join the general confusion of the homecoming celebration. "Come here! Let this old man give you a hug!" Mutti freed herself of her two youngest, and he embraced her.

"You must have put a word in for me. Did you?"

"Yes, I did, but why do you ask?"

"Well, this afternoon, just before my release, I was again questioned about my trip to Berlin. Today, however, the questioning session started out differently. 'You know Emil Schmidtke?' they asked me. That question made me think that you must have been in touch with them. I have a lot to tell you. That I am alive and here at home, though, is something I still can't comprehend. There are still more than twenty Germans in the jail. We can't forget them. We have to pray for them. You have no idea how they are suffering. Day and night the Russians showed us that they are the conquerors. They are using many tactics to demean us and avenge themselves. I'll tell you some things later. Right now I have to share the most exciting news ever with all of you. All the hardships I had to endure since I left here are overshadowed by the joyous news I got in Berlin."

"What news, Mutti?" Dieter asked quickly.

"I found out, Dieter, that your Vati is alive and well. He is in a prisoner of war camp in Africa. He was captured by the French in southern France and taken to a camp in Algeria. He is in the town of Gerryville, right at the edge of the Sahara Desert."

"How did you find that out, Emmy?" Kaetchen inquired.

"Well, that is a miracle, too. On the lampstand, at my aunt's house, I saw a small leaflet written by, of all people, our Pastor Walter from Insterburg. He has started organizing a search for his church members and calls for everyone from his congregation to get in touch with him. Since most families have been torn apart, he then helps reunite them. I immediately got in touch with him, and that is how I learned about Emil. Pastor Walter also informed me that Emil's best friend, Kurt, from the Insterburg choir, is in the same camp. It is strictly an officers' camp, and the French commander treats all the prisoners very well. Because the commander himself was once a prisoner in a German camp and was treated well, he is now repaying the Germans for their kindness to him. The prisoners are not allowed to work, so they just wile away their time. Vati apparently plays in a band and is organist at the camp church. The camp food is reported to be excellent. This exciting news and my experiences of the past few weeks make me even more determined to do everything possible to leave Lippehne. Our families have to be reunited. Our children have to have an education. This can never happen as long as we remain here. Before any more restrictions are put on us by this regime, we have to leave. We have to work hard for our freedom. There is no doubt about that, and we have to start immediately. The Lord has ways to get us out of here, and I know He is just waiting to show us His greatness again."

"You want us to leave Lippehne?" Dieter asked with a long face. "I like it here. I like this little farm. Where will we live when we leave here?"

"I don't know, my son, but I am positive that the Lord has a place for us somewhere."

"Will we eat potatoes there and drink milk?" my little sister wondered.

"We will have more to eat there than we have here, Pittimaus, and someday perhaps all your tummies will again be filled. The Berliners have ration cards. They get a little bread and a few grams of fat every day. Children are allotted some milk. It is still not enough to satisfy hungry stomachs, but it is quite an improvement over our situation."

"When will we leave the farm, Mutti?"

"I don't know, Dieter. Only the Lord has the answer to that question. We must pray diligently for His guidance and ask Him to show us very clearly when we shall make our move."

"What are the conditions like in the West, Emmy?" Onkel Emil asked.

"Because I have been there for only a few days, I can't tell you very much. I learned, however, that Germany has been divided into zones. Each zone is governed by a different nation. There is the American zone, the British zone, the French zone, and the Russian zone. The city of Berlin is also divided into four sectors. All the victors wanted a piece of that once glamorous city. Unfortunately, the war has stripped the city of all its glamor. From what I have seen, there is very little left except rubble. For three hours I climbed over ruins, broken glass, charred bricks, metal beams, and craters. It was quite rare to see a building that was still intact."

"How did you find your aunt's house, Emmy, in the midst of all that destruction?" Onkel Emil wondered.

"That was the most difficult part of my visit to Berlin. I asked people for directions to my aunt's street and usually they said, 'That street was totally destroyed' or 'I don't know.' People were just wandering aimlessly among the ruins, stooping occasionally to pick up a charred piece of wood that they would use for firewood, or looking in the ruins for something that might have escaped the flames. I saw only discouragement in those I met and talked to and soon found myself overcome by the same hopeless feeling. People live in holes to escape the elements. I saw one determined group of people, though. In spite of the terribly cold weather, they were working for a better future. They were cleaning bricks by using stones to beat the mortar off, then stacking them neatly into piles. That picture really touched my heart and exemplified the spirit of the German people. We can't sit by idly and do nothing about our destiny. We have to rise and help shape it ourselves and rebuild our country for us and our children.

"But I must get back to my story. When it began to get dark, I prayed really hard. 'Lord,' I said, 'please let me find my aunt's house. You lead the way. I am exhausted and at the end of my strength.' I stopped in my tracks, stood still, and began to scrutinize the area around me. I saw ruins, ruins, nothing but ruins. Then I looked behind me and saw part of one house. I even saw curtains in some of the windows. I braced myself, climbed over rubble to that partial building, and rang the door bell. And what do you think? Only our Lord can perform such a feat. My aunt opened the door! The remnants of her house resembled a small fortress in the midst of the ruins of Berlin. The sweet lady was shocked, yet glad to see me. We embraced and cried. She has suffered a lot during the bombing attacks. Her husband was killed one day before Germany capitulated. When the Russians invaded Berlin, they fell upon the surviving women, young and old, and disgraced everyone they could find.

"My aunt was brutally raped by a Russian youngster. Then the young soldier tried to wash himself in the toilet bowl, but the water continued to run out, so he then stuffed a towel in the hole to keep the water in. The Berliners have really endured much and have a difficult road ahead of them. Farther west, life is not much better because of the refugee problem. More than seven million people from the East are supposed to have fled to the West. By leaving their homes and farms, many tried to escape the deportations to Siberia; others were chased out of their homes by the Russians and the Poles. Those traveling people had been favorite targets of the enemies, however, as the Allies are now learning. Hundreds of thousands lost their lives on the open roads. Starvation, suicide, and sickness are continuing to kill thousands of those who survived. My aunt met a young refugee mother from Silesia combing through the ruins one day. She was scrounging around for food for her young daughter. Two days later, she met her again, and the two-year-old had died. In certain areas of the western and southern parts of Germany, some reconstruction is beginning, and the children have even returned to school."

"Does that mean that we have to go back to school when we go to the West?" Dieter broke in.

"Yes, my son. You see, if you want to make something of yourself, you have to have an education, and to get a good education, you have to return to school. I know you'd rather do all kinds of other exciting things instead of attending school, but to be properly prepared for life and get a good job when you are older, you have to acquire all the tools you can. You are a smart young man already, and because of it, I think you will find learning in a new school interesting and challenging."

"I hope you are right, Mutti."

Our devotional time was filled with praise and thanksgiving for Mutti's release. Then the little ones were tucked into bed and the rest of us gathered back into the living room to learn more about life outside of our little farm. In a few days we would have spent one year under the communist regime. We had not read one newspaper or heard one radio broadcast. We had not talked to one person who had been in the West, except Mutti. We had no idea where, aside from Vati, all of our relatives were. In the course of the year we had not had any mail. Vati's sister from America always wrote faithfully, and so did Vati. All of our friends knew that we had moved to Lippehne. Why had we had no letters from any of them? Why were we so isolated from the rest of world?

For the first time I began to realize what the isolation meant: it was being forced upon us. The war was over—it shouldn't have been necessary. Mutti was right. We had to leave. We had no freedom here at all.

"When we first left," Mutti continued, "we all felt that it would be safer to board the train from the next town, so we walked to the next railroad station. I wish that we had gotten off there on our return trip as well. But before I tell you what occurred in Lippehne, I'll start with our experiences after we left Berlin.

"As planned, the five of us met at the railroad station in Berlin at noon. We boarded the train to Kuestrin and moved slowly through destroyed towns and villages. Many times the train had to be rerouted because of broken tracks. Again, in a small village, among a field of rubble, people were cleaning bricks. This made me realize that Germany will some day rise above the ruins. In Kuestrin we had to change trains. We had all planned to jump the train before it came to a halt and quickly board the connecting one. But when we were ready to open the car door, we noticed Russians running along both sides of the train. 'Get down! Down on the floor!' our neighbor commanded, and we all dropped to the floor. All the other passengers did the same. When the train stopped, we remained on the floor.

"Suddenly the doors were forced open and Russians stomped into the car. They told us to get up and pushed us out of the door. Screaming and hollering, they herded all of us to their headquarters. No one was allowed to talk. All of our papers and tickets were taken away. 'You spies! You spies!' they yelled and shoved about twenty of us into a small room, which was furnished with only a few chairs and a table. I don't know what I would have done had I not felt the Lord's closeness at that moment. I thought about Emil and the children, and the seriousness of my situation began to overwhelm me. But then that still, sweet voice said: 'I will guide thee. Don't be afraid. Don't fear for your family. They are in my loving care. Lean on me, my child.' How sweetly He talked to me and gave me His peace.

"When it was dark, some of us placed our heads on the table and tried to sleep. But our neighbor began to whisper, 'We must escape. I have checked things out. There are only two Russians guarding us, and they are busy with their vodka bottles. They will be totally drunken shortly. Then we will sneak past them and start running.' About ten minutes later, she and I were the first to escape. We slowly opened the door and tiptoed past the sleeping guards out of the building. Just as we had reached a hedgerow, we heard the soldiers yelling and knew our escape attempt had been unsuccessful. The moonlight and the freshly fallen snow made it very easy for them to track us. Our neighbor told them in Russian that we had to go to the bathroom, and that was true, too, but they chased us back into that room. I put my head on the table and fell asleep. Then something jolted me out of my deep sleep. It was our neighbor again. 'Let's go,' she said. 'The guards are stone drunk and sleeping.' She and I left the room and started running toward the ruins of Kuestrin. We zigzagged like rabbits for a while to confuse the Russians in case they pursued us."

"Excuse me, Emmychen," Kaetchen interrupted, "the guards were so drunk that they never noticed you were leaving?"

"Yes, they were so inebriated that they never opened their eyes as we were sneaking past them. Three other women of our group and others from our room had also escaped and stumbled through the ruins as fast as possible. All of a sudden, though, we heard soldiers yelling and knew immediately they had detected our escape. We continued to run and then threw ourselves into a ditch near the railroad tracks. In our fright we did not realize that we had thrown ourselves into a ditch of water and ice. We thought it was just snow. For about seven miles we crawled along the ditch parallel to the tracks. We were wet and frozen through and through. When we came to a railroad station, we all decided to drop our earlier plans of walking to Lippehne and instead take a train. Fortunately we didn't have to wait long before one arrived. As we jumped on, I was praying that the conductor would somehow forget to ask for our tickets because we didn't have any, and the Lord again answered my prayer. I suggested to the others to leave the train one stop before Lippehne and walk home. Somehow I sensed that things would not go well there, but I was outvoted by my companions. Because they were all cold and anxious to get home, they wanted to stay on the train. I submitted to their wishes, and we were all captured in Lippehne. Tomorrow I'll tell you about my jail experience. Now I really have to go to bed and get some sleep."

"I don't blame you, Emmy," Kaetchen agreed. "You have gone through a lot."

"And all of this because of one man! Hitler!" Onkel Emil added. "Germans are chased, herded, raped, molested, and killed, long after the war has ended! We just had no idea what life is like outside of Lippehne. I had thought, however, that it was better than your description of it. You are right, Emmy! We will not sit here in isolation and hope for an improvement. That may never come. We have to leave here, and we have to leave soon."

As we went upstairs, Mutti placed her arm around my shoulders. How wonderful it was to be near her! I was so thankful tonight. Mutti was at home! Vati was well! But when I thought of what she had gone through—crawling in a ditch, being wet and cold and hungry—I wanted to cry.

"Good night, Schaefle! Thank you for taking my place while I was gone. You did a wonderful job." Mutti kissed me.

My brothers and sister were exuberant throughout the next day. Mutti was home! They were constantly hugging her.

"Schaefle, would you and Dieter please grind some millet for me? I need to cook some soup," Mutti told us.

When I watched Mutti prepare the soup and sweeten it with a little of our syrup, I sensed an urgency in the way she did it. I also noticed that later, when she sewed, she did it differently somehow. The needle seemed to fly faster than ever.

"I am starting to sew for our freedom, Schaefle," she told me when I asked her why there was such a difference in her actions. "With the Lord's help, we will leave soon. I have to make up for lost time and finish some of these projects so that we can get money to buy bread."

Would I have time for some knitting today? I hadn't touched the socks I was working on for a long time. I wished I could spend one whole day just knitting, but it didn't seem likely that I would any time soon. I kept dreaming about it, though, and whenever I knitted, I thought of Omi. She taught me so much. She had taught me how to shape the heel of a sock and how to knit double with one thread. "This gives the sock extra warmth and strength," she explained. I also thought of the wonderful time we always had in her garden in Insterburg. We played in the gazebo and almost touched the sky on the swing Opi had built especially for us children.

One day when I was on the swing, Opi had killed some chickens and roosters in the backyard. Suddenly a beheaded rooster began flying straight toward me. I screamed and ducked, almost falling off the swing. Opi recaptured his dinner and began plucking the beautiful feathers. Yes, I liked all the memories. But what had become of my sweet Omi? Where was Mutti's sister-in-law? Had Omi survived the trip out of Lippehne on that cold day? As days slipped into the past, all of our questions remained unanswered.

Mutti's heart was often broken when we talked about her parents on the farm in Heydekrug, East Prussia, and her ninety-three-year-old grandfather. Were they still alive? Would we ever see them again? "We'll see them in heaven, if not here on earth," Mutti said. "They are all believers in the Lord Jesus."

At times I couldn't bear the thought of possibly not ever seeing them here on earth, and I felt especially sorry for my youngest brother. Would he miss out on so much? Would Udo never know how much fun it was to build sand castles on the sandy river bank, right next to their farm? Would he never swim there and take boat trips? Would he never ride high atop the hay wagons or drive to church in the black and yellow horse-drawn carriage? Would he never be bundled up and cozy under blankets and sit next to the Schiller Omi on the sleigh when she goes to town? Would he never hear the ringing of the bells that were fastened to the horses' harnesses and see the beautiful horses move into a trot, pulling the sleigh to church? Would Udo never smell the freshly rendered honey from Opi's hives? Would he never play in the hayloft? Would he never sit at the long table in the living room and hear Opi read the Bible and Omi play the guitar? Would he never sit on his great-grandfather's lap, look at his smile, twinkling eyes, and curly gray hair? Would he never take a walk with him across the meadows and watch the storks in the fields? As I dug into the files of my memory, I considered myself unbelievably rich, and I hoped that Udo would someday have the same wonderful memories of his grandparents and the wonderful ways in which they shared their lives with him. Was it possible that some day everything would again be as I knew it, or would our memories be the only link to the past of which the war could not deprive us?

16
The Russian Jail

It was quiet on our little farm. The children were sleeping, and darkness had drawn the rest of us into the living room to learn more about Mutti's experiences.

"Liane and Dieter told you how our capture at the railroad station was carried out. They also must have told you how they followed us until the Russians became angry and chased them away. You have no idea how difficult it was for me to see my children cry and not be able to touch or comfort them. Well, after Dieter and Liane left, all those taken captive that afternoon had to line up outside. Under guard, we had to stand at attention some distance from one another and were not allowed to talk. Frozen through and through, my clothes and shoes still wet, we stood in the cold for hours. The first one to be called in for questioning was our neighbor. When she passed me, she mumbled through her teeth, 'I'll get you all out.' She must have thought she would be able to accomplish that with her knowledge of the Russian language. The cold began to numb my legs and hands and I wanted to stomp my feet to get the circulation back, but that was not permitted. We were standing there, suffering from the winter's chills when I suddenly noticed our neighbor strutting out of the building. She held her head high and didn't even glance at us, for she had gained her freedom. I was the last one to be called into headquarters. Four officers with stern faces were firing questions at me. 'Why did you go to Berlin? What did you do there? How long were you there? Where do your relatives live?' Dozens of other questions were hurled at me. Many were nothing but traps, but the Lord gave me wisdom to recognize them and not fall into them."

"Did they speak through an interpreter?" Onkel Emil wondered.

"No, one of the officers spoke German fluently. Over and over I told them that I had visited my aunt to see if she had any idea where my husband was. My four children need their father. We have been separated during the war, I told them. Constantly they yelled, 'You spy! You spy!' Nothing I said convinced them otherwise. Finally they confiscated my handbag and rucksack and motioned for two guards to take me away. They led me through several dark corridors, opened a door, and pushed me down the steps into a dark cellar.

"When I got to the bottom of the steps, a clammy, strange odor reached my nose. I stood still, listened into the darkness, and realized immediately that I was not alone. The air was cold and damp, but I could hear several women sobbing. I asked who else was present. Quite a few names were called out, including the names of my travel companions—our neighbor, of course, was not there. Then I asked them why they were crying. That question made the sobbing increase. 'Well,' I said, 'I see the captors have accomplished what they set out to do. I, for one, will not give them the satisfaction of seeing me cry. Crying does not help our situation at all. There is only One who can ease our pain right now, and that is the Lord Jesus Christ.' Then I explained to them how they can get peace and comfort through Him."

"I am glad you could be a witness for the Lord right there in the jail cell, Emmy," Onkel Emil rejoiced.

"Yes, Emil. I had quite a few opportunities to speak of the Lord. We began to feel our way around the dark room and found rough boards nailed to the wall near the window, which consisted of iron bars rather than glass. That explained why it was so cold in the room. We climbed on top of the high wooden planks, and huddled close to each other to get some warmth, but even in that position we shivered when the icy winds from the lake blew over our bodies. No matter what we tried, it was impossible to get warm without blankets. We attempted to sleep. Some of us had almost succeeded, but were suddenly awakened when the door above the steps was kicked open. Boisterous guards ordered us to get out of the cellar. Quickly we slid off our boards and felt our way up the steps.

"We were herded outdoors—there were about twenty-five of us—and forced to line up, standing at attention. To keep us alert, the guards constantly cracked their whips. Their attempt to frighten us that way was successful, I suppose. I shivered so hard that I believe you could actually see my body shaking. One row to my right, I noticed someone bending back and forth like a tree in a storm. The crack of a whip brought that poor prisoner back to reality again, and she managed to stand still for a short time. Several of the prisoners from the other cells were men. After about two hours of standing in the snow and being whipped by icy winds, we were chased back into the cold cellar. In our cell, we again climbed on top of the scaffolding, longing for warmth and sleep. We had hardly settled down when we were driven outside once more to stand in the cold for two hours to be 'counted.' By the time we returned from our second line-up, none of us were capable of remaining awake for another minute. Most of us were just beginning to fall asleep when gun butts were again beating against our door. It was still pitch-dark and we, along with the other prisoners, had to go to the dining hall for breakfast, which consisted of one slice of dark bread and one cup of malt coffee. The coffee was only lukewarm and didn't do much to give us warmth.

"As soon as we had finished eating, the guards hollered, 'Daway rabotay! Daway rabotay!' The men were given the task of felling the trees around the headquarters' compound, and we women had to saw them into firewood. The saws were terribly dull, but that didn't matter to our captors. With the Russians standing over us, we had to struggle. If we didn't work fast enough to suit them, they pushed the end of their rifle barrels into our bodies to remind us that they were the ones who held our lives in their hands. Finally it was dinner time. The exhausting work had warmed us up and made us hungry, too. We were led to the dining hall for a bowl of watery soup. The Russians told us Germans to go to the end of the line. Their friends, the Polish prisoners, would eat first. But they did more than eat! When they had finished ladling their soup, they all took turns spitting into the soup. 'Now you eat, you German pigs,' they sneered. None of us touched that soup. We all turned around and left the hall hungry."

"So you all worked hard all day and ate nothing?" I asked.

"That's right. Could any of you have eaten that soup? Schaefle, I normally would not tell this next experience in your presence, but you have seen so much in the past one and a half years that I know the next story will probably not shock or surprise you. So I'll let you stay up a little longer to hear this, too. Or would you like to go to bed now?"

"No, Mutti. I'd like to stay. I probably can't sleep tonight anyway when I think of all the suffering you went through."

"All right then, Schaefle. Well, the Russians were absolutely furious with us Germans for daring to refuse the soup they had provided and came up with an idea to further humiliate and punish us. Ten of us women had to stand in a circle in the dining hall. Then they pushed a nude Polish man into the center of the circle. 'He many lice,' one of the guards shouted. 'You woman pick lice.' Nobody moved. The guard repeated the command. Again nobody moved. Then he stared at each of us. When he fastened his eyes on me, I prayed: 'Lord help!' Instantly I sensed a calm flooding my soul. I stepped forward and said, 'We are German women. We refuse to do anything that dirty.' He must have understood me very well, and that defiance caused him to blow up. 'You woman pick lice,' he repeated. I again told him we would not do that. His face turned bright red; he stepped forward and aimed his rifle at me. I expected him to shoot me. Instead, he suddenly stepped back, became silent, and made us stand in that circle for what seemed like an eternity. None of us looked at the poor shivering Polish man. When the guards deemed our punishment sufficient, they chased us outside again to saw and chop wood. After sawing wood until evening, we were herded inside again. On the way in, we grabbed some snow, when the guards were not watching, and did what was strictly forbidden; we washed ourselves—I guess I didn't mention yet that our bathroom facility consisted of only one bucket in our cell.

"In the building, they took us to the dining hall and gave us one slice of dark bread and one cup of lukewarm malt coffee. At night, everybody in our cell was exhausted physically and mentally. Several were ready to explode from anger and hatred. I suggested that we sing to keep up our spirits. So we softly sang hymns and folk songs. But as soon as the guards heard the singing, they ordered us to be quiet. By that time even the slow followers had noticed the calming effect of the singing, and they continued with the rest of us in a whisper tone. When we were almost settled on our boards and ready to doze off, the first night's procedure was repeated. We were chased out of the cellar, and lined up outside. The whips were cracked, and we were not allowed to move. This night, however, was much colder than the previous night. A fierce wind was whipping across the lake. Even the guards in their long, heavy coats and fur hats seemed to be freezing. They just let us stand there while they went into the building. The minute they left, I was confronted with a new problem—escape. This was a perfect time to escape. The guards were inside. The night was clear and bright. The lake was frozen and just a few feet away, and I still had strength to run. If the guards remained inside for a while, I thought I could make it. But then, suddenly, something suppressed my wonderful escape thoughts—the snow. Tracking me would have been too easy, and flying bullets have no obstacles on the lake. They would not have any trouble hitting me. And what would my four children do without me? My heartbeat slowed down and I said, 'Lord, You brought me here for a reason, and I trust You to get me out of this situation. Please help me. Amen.' Instead of running, I continued to pray and work my feet into a stomping rhythm that revitalized my whole body. Even though I was still chilled, I felt an extra surge of strength—supernatural strength. About two hours later we were chased back into our cells, where we again groped for sleep and warmth."

"Emmychen, I just can't fathom what you have gone through," Kaetchen admitted, "but I still want to hear more of your story."

"The next morning after breakfast, I was given a very special assignment. A guard led me alone to the Russians' personal restroom. 'Rabotay! Rabotay!' he yelled with a mean look on his face as he pointed at the feces piled all around the toilet seats. The sight of it made me gag. 'Rabotay! Rabotay!' he continued hollering. I looked around for a bucket or brush but found none. I wanted to search in other rooms for a bucket, but he did not let me. Then I went outside to get snow, and with my bare hands and the snow I cleaned that human dung. The Lord was good to me by keeping me strong and not permitting me to faint from that horrible sight and the stench. After I had finished, I walked past the guard, went outside, and did the forbidden thing again: I washed my hands with snow. He didn't say anything but chased me back to saw and split logs.

"Our noon meal was again mixed with Polish spittle, and we all refused to eat the soup. While standing in the soup line, I saw a most horrible sight—a male German skeleton with a buttonless shirt, light pants, and blue, bare feet in wooden sandals. He was trying to balance himself while waiting for his meal. One of his friends whispered to me, 'His feet are blue up to his ankles because they are frost-damaged. He also has dysentery. He is in a single cell right next to ours, without a bed or blanket. Every morning guards take him to the lake where he has to chop a hole in the ice, take off his soiled pants, wash them, and put them back on.' "

"That poor man," I interrupted. "Dieter and I thought all those holes were made by ice fishermen."

"No, Schaefle. There is one hole in the ice for every day of that man's suffering. But he is no longer chopping ice. He died."

For a while we sat in utter silence. My thoughts were on that man. Did he have a family and children? Might something terrible be happening to Vati right now? Was life really worth living? How could everyone here still talk about a loving God?

"Emmychen," Kaetchen said, "why is all this happening to our people? What have we done to deserve this? What was that man's crime?"

"The righteous Judge knows," Onkel Emil answered. "He will let justice prevail some day. We don't have to worry about that. I am glad He knows about our future, too. If we didn't have that assurance, life would be utterly hopeless. Your story, Emmy, is incredible. You poor woman! What you have gone through! Even though it is late and we are all tired, I would still like to hear the rest of your jail experiences."

"I am rather tired, too, but I'll finish. Well, those first three days as a prisoner seemed like an eternity, the nights especially.

On the morning of the fourth day, the lady cook went around the jail to look for two women to help her in the kitchen. You can't imagine how overjoyed I was when she selected me as one of the two. The thought of working in the warm kitchen and perhaps getting more to eat was absolutely thrilling. Escaping the guards was even more exciting. Our first assignment on the kitchen crew was to scrub the dining hall, several adjacent rooms, and the kitchen. We were all getting rather weak from working so hard and eating only two slices of bread per day. Scrubbing and scraping the thick filth on the floors took a lot of strength and patience, but the Lord graciously provided those. We laughed out loud when we discovered an inlaid floor underneath all that dirt."

"You were not punished for laughing?" I asked.

"No, they must not have heard us. After the kitchen was scrubbed and polished, the cook, a kindhearted Polish lady, decided to keep me on as her permanent helper. When we were alone and no guards were in sight, she always handed me something to eat. She, of course, was not allowed to do that, but she risked getting caught to help me. It was absolutely wonderful to be in a warm kitchen from morning till evening. At night I had to return to the cell to try to keep warm. Always, we had to line up outside at least twice for several hours during the night, but I would then return to the kitchen the next morning. All of my cellmates envied me. How they wished they, too, could work in a warm place and get more to eat. The Lord has been good to me. But with the life of ease I now enjoyed, a new problem arose. It was lice. Since we had to eat, sleep, and work in the same clothes without personal hygiene, those little troublemakers spread like wildfire and infested all of us. Scratching was useless and required too much energy. So we all just suffered while they multiplied."

"As I was rolling out pastries in the kitchen, a Russian officer entered. He came toward me and asked, 'You know Emil Schmidtke? You live in Luisenstrasse? You mother have four children?' When I answered 'yes' to all those questions, he growled, 'Woman, come.' Fear overcame me. I became almost paralyzed, my mind racing. How could I escape? I was not going to let them rape me. 'Lord, help!' He raised his voice and repeated his command: 'Woman come.' I still didn't move until he added, 'You go home.' "

"Had I heard him correctly? Go home? The cook got the message before I did. She threw her arms around me and said,

'No! No! No!' but the officer waited for me to follow him for more questioning. Three officers again bombarded me with questions, but they must have realized that there were no deviations from my earlier answers. Then they winked at one another, returned my purse and rucksack, and without a word gestured for me to leave. I didn't look behind me but almost floated down the street. Thank you, Lord! That was all I could think of at the time. And here I am! The bedtime story is over."

"Before we retire, though, I want to thank you again, Emil, for working so diligently for my release. The Russians really must have high regard for you and your work. They would not have freed me otherwise. And, Kaetchen, thank you again for watching over my children so beautifully. To you, Schaefle, a bouquet of roses, but since I don't have roses, a big hug and a kiss is what I'll give you with all my love."

17
Improvements

"**K**aetchen," Mutti said one morning, several weeks later, "Liane told me that we have a small grocery store in town now. I think I'll take my silver dishes and linens and see if I can trade them in for food. I am so glad the Lord allowed me that one trip back to Insterburg right after we moved here to salvage some of our belongings. It is a miracle, too, that the Russians have never found the dark, wet basement here under the kitchen floor. I have the feeling that those things down there will be the means of our future survival."

While Kaetchen and I finished the laundry, Mutti went to the grocery store to barter her wedding gifts and hand-embroidered linens for food. Our scrubbing boards were barely put away when she returned with a whole bag of groceries.

"The owner of the store, a Polish lady, was so excited about all my treasures," Mutti announced. "She gave me 10,000 zlotys. Come and see all the things I bought! Here are two loaves of bread, half a pound of butter, half a pound of sugar, some salt, one potato for each person, and a little black tea for you, Kaetchen. Tomorrow the children can go and buy some milk."

"Emmychen, I know all the things you took are worth much more and can't ever be paid for in food or money. But in times of starvation there is absolutely nothing worth more than food."

"You are right, Kaetchen. If I think about all the years it took me to do all that handwork, I get sick about it. But how could I hold on to things of the past while my children are starving to death?"

"The barber shop will be open in a few moments," Mutti informed all the members of our household after dinner. "Everyone in need of a professional haircut, please meet in the kitchen. We cut hair on even the smallest heads as you well know, and we start with the youngest and cut our way up to the oldest." And with that remark she gave Onkel Emil a funny look.

"You know I don't like to be last."

"And that is exactly why I said that," she chuckled. "It is too difficult to work on little boys while they are half asleep. So you'll just have to be last."

Finally Onkel Emil's turn came, and while he was sitting under Mutti's scissors, he told those of us who were watching about the latest happenings at the tailor shop.

"The two women who went to Berlin with you, Emmy, were released from jail last night. I hardly recognized them when they reported for work this morning. They look so old and haggard. The six weeks of hard labor and little food have really taken a toll on them. They don't look as if they can live very long. They are just skin and bones. I continually thank the Lord for having set you free so quickly. Where would I go for my haircut if you were too weak to give me one?"

"Is that all you can think about, Emil?" Mutti said with a little bite in her words.

"Now, Emmy, you mustn't be so touchy. Can't you take a bit of humor anymore? We have to keep up our spirits. We have to be able to have a sense of humor—if we don't, we are emotionally defeated."

"You are right, Emil. I'm sorry. It's just that my thoughts were on those two women you described. I could have been one of them who had to suffer so long. Why is the Lord so good to me?" There were no answers to those kinds of questions. I wondered, often, myself why we were all still alive and relatively healthy when according to statistics and human reasoning, we should all have been dead long ago.

"You children really play well together," Kaetchen remarked as Mutti was cleaning up the barbershop. "It is a joy for me to see that. What are you playing today?"

"We are playing post office, Mutti," Hanno said. "Dieter is the clerk behind the window, Marlies is the cleaning lady, I am sorting the mail, Vilmar is the mailman, and Liane is watching."

"Well, that is really nice. You are well organized: everyone has an exciting job to do, and no one is left out. It must bring joy to the heart of our Lord to see you getting along so well. Now, since I am here, does my little mailman have a letter for me?"

"Yes, Mutti," Vilmar said excitedly. "I have two letters for you. One, two," he counted as he handed them to Kaetchen.

"I have seen that one letter many times before. It is one of those old letters that always shows up during post office play time. But this one is new to me. Where did you children get this? Where did it come from?"

"I don't know, Mutti. It was just lying on the floor in the hallway this morning."

No one knew anything about this mysterious piece of mail.

"The writing is unfamiliar," Kaetchen continued, "and so is the sender. But it is addressed to me. That means I can open it." She turned the letter over and again read the address. Finally she pushed her small finger in the flap and ripped it open.

"The first page seems to be written in Polish. Why would anyone write to me in Polish?" Baffled by this question, she rushed to Mutti. "Look at this letter, Emmy! The children were playing with it."

"Is the second page written in Polish, too?" Mutti asked. Kaetchen glanced at the backside of the page.

"Oh, no! Look at this! It says Wilhelm Mecklenburg, Bochum, Germany. What does all this mean? Does it mean that Wilhelm lives in Bochum? Just where did this letter come from? I'm going over to the Polish preacher and let him translate it for me." In seconds Kaetchen was ready to leave for the preacher's house.

A short while later she returned, feet hardly touching the ground as she flew into the house. "Listen, everybody! Listen!

Another miracle! Wilhelm is well! He is pastor of a church in Bochum. Can you believe it? Thank you, Lord! Thank you, Lord!" Kaetchen was nearly beside herself with joy. "He met the man who wrote this letter in his church. He was someone's guest there and played the violin for one of the services. When Wilhelm found out that this Christian had connections in Poland, he asked him to send his address to his friends and from there on to us. It simply boggles my mind to think that we received it. Only the Lord knows how it got here. We have a great God! Wilhelm is alive and well!" And she danced around the kitchen singing: " 'This is the day which the Lord has made; we will rejoice and be glad in it.' This is just the boost I need to carry on. Wilhelm is alive! Hanno! Vilmar! Your daddy is alive and well! Praise be to His wonderful Name! My husband is alive!"

The rejoicing continued long after Onkel Emil had returned from work.

"Thank you all for your prayers!" Kaetchen was still overflowing with joy.

Deep in thought and sad-looking, Onkel Emil quietly limped into the living room. He was the only one who had not yet heard from his life's partner.

It was only a few days later that his sadness increased even more. "The final purging is occurring," he reported sadly after returning from work.

"What do you mean by that, Emil?"

"A Russian officer came to the tailor shop today to announce that all of my seamstresses and their families have to leave Lippehne tomorrow. They must leave. No one is given a choice. Our neighbor is also among them. 'Don't ask any questions—just leave or we make you wish you had left,' they were told. 'You and your family stay,' the officer told me sternly. 'You are not allowed to go. We need you.' I told him that I can't do the job alone. 'We send Polish women. You train Polish women,' and with that he left the shop."

"What an opportunity that would have been for us to get across the border," Mutti said. "Our time to leave must not have come yet. The Lord must have a better way for us than 'walking' toward freedom."

"Do you know what this new development means for us?" Onkel Emil asked. "It means that we are the only Germans left

172

in the town of Lippehne. We are the only ones of a population of 20,000. What is the Lord trying to tell us? Why is He keeping us here? Again we have to look to the future for our answers. Some things we will not understand until we get to eternity. It was just heart-rending to see my co-workers get that terrible news. Most of them are mothers with children, and some still have their elderly parents living with them. None of them have Polish money to purchase train tickets. We have to pray hard for all of them."

"Yes," Kaetchen said, "and we have to pray that it will not be too cold for those poor folks tomorrow. Physically, I know I could not survive such a trip. I just don't feel strong enough anymore."

"Now, Kaetchen!" Mutti said as if to scold her. "We will not let discouragement grip our hearts, will we? Discouragement is not of the Lord! You know that! Our Lord always says: 'Be of a good courage! Be not dismayed!' Be strong! Be not afraid! We can't be faint-hearted. We have to keep our minds stayed on Him continually. We can't look at our frail bodies and waning strength. The Lord is our strength! He is our Rock! He will help us, right? We have to be emotionally strong for our children, for each other, for the sake of our mates. We can't permit discouragement to take hold of us. We have not suffered nearly as much as some. The Lord's desire is for us to worship Him and not complain as did the children of Israel in the Bible."

"You are right, Emmy! Thank you for setting me straight! I don't know what I'd do without you and your friendship."

"I consider you my dear friend, too, Kaetchen. And that is why it troubles me to see you downcast."

Mutti then proceeded to practice her optimistic spirit by drilling us on Vati's homecoming poems. Did she really think we'd forget if we didn't recite them every single day? Or did she want us to be reminded of Vati through our recital sessions? It became boring for me to recite so often, but when I saw her gentle smile of approval and her beautiful, dreamy eyes, I realized how difficult life must have been for her without her husband. Then I became ashamed of my feelings of rebellion. Thank you, Lord, for such a wonderful and courageous mother, I thought to myself, and then I recited my poem.

"Honey! We have a jar of honey!" Mutti announced. "What a delicacy! A customer gave me honey instead of money today."

We hadn't tasted honey in more than a year. It always used to be our favorite spread. One of Mutti's friends, her Polish customer, brought us a jar. Oh, how I had always enjoyed honey! My love had been started at my grandparents' farm. Dieter and I would always watch Mutti's father gather the honey from his hives. Then he would put the honeycombs in the separator, and Dieter and I were allowed to crank the wooden handle. Opi was seldom stung by his bees because they knew him. But Mutti's brother was once attacked by a swarm. Covered with them from head to toe, he raced down to the river, screaming in agony, and dived into the water. When he came back to the surface, he watched hundreds of bees struggling for their lives, but his life was saved.

"Everybody, please line up," Mutti instructed. "The Lord has given us a very special gift today. We have one jar of honey. Each man—we have only one—woman, and child will today be able to enjoy one teaspoonful of honey. In three days each one will be given another spoonful."

My mouth was beginning to water as I saw Mutti dipping the spoon into the thick, golden mass. Honey! What a treat! I used to take the enjoyment of eating honey for granted. I used to take many things for granted now that I thought of it. I never considered food anything special. We always had plenty of it. Udo pulled up his nose when he tasted the sticky substance. He acted as if he was eating something sour.

"It is so sweet!" Marlies exclaimed.

"Did bees make this honey?" little Vilmar asked with his eyes widening.

"Yes, my son. They did."

"How, Mutti, how do they do it?"

While everyone was still smacking and licking his lips, Kaetchen gathered the children around her and tried to explain how bees manufacture honey.

"Honeybees collect honey from trees, flowers, bushes, and blooming weeds. They fly into fields, woods, gardens, and just about anywhere they can find nectar. They especially like clover, heather, and linden blossoms. They collect the honey from the plants and take it to their hives so that they have food for all the thousands of bees in the hive during the long winter months."

"Do bees eat honey, too?"

174

"Yes, Vilmar, they do. But they usually have much more than they need. So the beekeeper takes the extra honey out of the hive and uses it himself or sells it. That is how we got this honey. It was bought, and then Tante Emmy's customer gave it to her. Each little bee makes only about one teaspoonful of honey in its life. Can you imagine how many bees the Lord needed to make one whole jar full of honey?"

"Very, very many," Hanno answered.

"Very, very, very many," Marlies added.

Onkel Emil went through many struggles in the next weeks to rebuild the tailor shop. The new personnel consisted of Polish women. Communicating with them was the major problem. After a few days, however, he was once again singing when he came home from work. He had been a soloist in several operas, and music was still his passion. He was always in a good mood when the house resounded with his tenor voice. Even Russian officers were fascinated with his voice—a group had once requested one day that he sing part of an opera for them.

The Polish preacher told Kaetchen that he planned to start the church services again. He had been meeting with just a few people at a time during the winter months. The meetings were held in different homes. No one had advance notice of where they would be. Keeping the get-togethers a secret from the government was of utmost importance. Now that spring was here and warmer weather was to begin, the meetings would occasionally be held at the cemetery.

Many other things weighed on our minds during those days, though. It became increasingly more difficult for Dieter and me to find firewood. After a stormy night we would leave the house as soon as daylight broke, but we seldom found much. The old Polish ladies usually met us with large bundles of sticks that they had gathered in the middle of the night. The charcoal supply was also dwindling. There were still charred beams in the top of some of the buildings, but it was definitely too dangerous for us to climb up there. The eight sacks of coal that Kaetchen had sifted out of rubble and ashes near the hospital one day and brought home were also used up.

"Lord, send a big storm that will make big limbs fall out of the trees," Onkel Emil prayed one day, "or send us a warm spring early." Meanwhile, we were looking toward new ways of building up our food supply. Kaetchen returned to her father's old garden plot to try to clean it up and get it ready for planting some vegetables.

"Can you imagine, Emmychen, what a Polish woman told me while I was in the garden today?"

It was one of the few times I ever saw Kaetchen truly angry.

"She said 'Why are you so foolish to do all that work? You won't be allowed to stay here and harvest it anyway. You will be chased out just like the rest of the Germans.' "

"She was that brazen?"

"Yes! Who was she to tell me what I could or couldn't do in my dad's garden? That really made my blood boil. They just come here and take everything from us and then keep rubbing it in."

"Yes, Kaetchen," Mutti said. "I can imagine how you must have wanted to lash out. I don't blame you for becoming angry. But at least you did not lose your life because of your anger. Do you remember the man here in Lippehne who had just finished building his house after years of work? Because he didn't want the Russians to have it, he, in his anger, destroyed it and the Russians shot him."

"I remember."

"I think we are learning that a war doesn't bring out the best in people. I don't think we really understand our innermost being until we are in the grip of war and hatred. How would we ever know what we are capable of doing? How would we ever know how much suffering we can endure? When we sit in nice, warm homes with our families, enjoying a life of ease, we can't fathom the real war that can be fought within one's body and soul."

"You are absolutely right, Emmychen. I never thought about that."

18
Tickets to Freedom

The weather did grow warmer. It brought not only promises of warm spring, but another exciting possibility. We first sensed the change one day when Mutti came home, appearing to be floating on air. Of course, we wanted to know what had happened, but she wouldn't tell us. "I will tell you all later. All I can say is that I sense something good might come our way."

No guessing helped. Not even Kaetchen could find out what the secret was. Mutti remained firm.

"I will tell all of you after dinner. Onkel Emil has to be here, too."

Before we settled down for our devotional, she finally shared the cause of her excitement with us. "You all know my Polish customer and friend. And you know that she has come over regularly to check on my sewing and sometimes just to visit. She speaks German beautifully, and I am learning Polish from her. So in the course of time we have become well acquainted. One day I happened to tell her of my hopes and dreams for our future, and she promised me that she would do anything she could to help us leave Lippehne. Until today she has been completely silent on that subject, and, therefore, I thought that she was not serious about her offer. I also couldn't imagine how she could be of help to us. Today, however, she made me aware of the fact that she has been working quietly on our behalf. She told me the Polish district magistrate went on vacation, and his assistant is a good friend of hers. She has talked to her friend, and he will give us authorization papers to leave Lippehne— for 10,000 zlotys. After my initial shock and joy wore off, I informed her that we would really have to think about the offer. Also we don't have that sum of money. 'I'll buy your sewing machine for 10,000 zlotys,' she said. That didn't surprise me because I knew she has had her eye on my machine for a long time. She was always fascinated by it. I told her once that she could have it for her efforts should we leave Lippehne.

"Anyway, I wasn't sure what to tell her. The thought of perhaps leaving caused my whole being to jump with joy. But the ethical question crept up—could the Lord use these means to get us out of Lippehne? What do you think?"

Both Kaetchen and Onkel Emil were unusually quiet for a long time. Finally Onkel Emil broke the stillness by saying, "That is bribery."

"Yes," Kaetchen added, propping her chin on her hand, "can something wrong be used to give us the desires of our heart? Can this be of the Lord? That is a difficult question."

All through the evening the adults tried to answer the question. Was this of the Lord?

"We all have to pray constantly and diligently until the Lord gives us an answer," Mutti suggested. "Humanly speaking, this sounds like a great opportunity to gain our freedom. But is this the Lord's will?"

The prayers that night were pleas for God's wisdom. "Please, Lord, help us to make the decision that is in accordance with Your will. Show us very clearly what You want us to do. We don't want to stray from Your guidance and Your will for our lives. Please, help us, Lord!" Each one of us spent much time in personal prayer that Thursday night.

Early Friday morning Mutti's friend knocked excitedly on the front door. Onkel Emil had not yet left for work. "All the paper work will be done for you," she told everybody. "Your train leaves from Lippehne at six o'clock on Sunday morning. You will have to leave here at five o'clock, while it is still somewhat

178

dark, so that nobody will see you. My friend himself will come to your house on Saturday night and bring you the papers and tickets." She then wished us a good day and left.

"Let's pray hard," Onkel Emil said, closing the front door behind him as he left for work.

"What do you think, Emmy? Shall we start packing while we pray? This might just be another disappointment. But, I think we have learned that we should pray more."

"I agree, Kaetchen. I think we should do as you suggest; pack and pray. Since our hopes have been dashed before, we can't get them up too high—Kaetchen! I just had a terrible thought! What if this offer is a trap the magistrate is luring us into? If we go along with his plans, we can be accused of wrongdoing, and who knows what he'll do to us then? But on the other hand, I don't think my friend is that kind of person. I think she is sincere and really wants to help us."

"There are many instances in the Bible, Emmy, in which the Lord uses the enemies to help His people. He, of course, can do that in our case, too. Maybe this is not a setup, but His divine leading." The day flew by, even though we had a lot on our minds, because we all kept very busy.

"What have you ladies been doing all day today while the man of the house was working?" Onkel Emil asked teasingly when he came in from work.

"Well," Mutti said, "we have just been twiddling our thumbs while waiting for the master of the house to return. And now that he is here, we shall continue to do so while he sits down and tells us what he has accomplished today."

"This man has kept a lot of Polish women busy—quite a feat in itself. Only a few speak a little German, and the Polish words I have acquired don't seem to help much. So we all just muddle through the day and try to achieve our common goal of making uniforms for the Russians. Most of the women despise the Russians because they forced them out of their homeland to come to Lippehne. Right now I can't imagine how those two peoples will ever live harmoniously.

"A few of the women have sewing experience, but the rest are novices. It is difficult so far to get much productivity out of them. I have tried to work ahead on some cutting and several other jobs, so that they can continue without me for a while . . . in other words, I have begun to make preparations in case we should decide to leave on Sunday. But now I want to know, all jesting aside, what you ladies did today aside from praying."

"We packed," Kaetchen replied.

"Does that mean you think it is the Lord's will for us to leave?"

"We don't know, but Emmy and I decided to pack and pray. We want to be prepared in case the Lord says: 'This is it! Go!' We have placed the situation completely in the Lord's hands. If the assistant magistrate really comes with the departure permits tomorrow night, I think we can consider it His will. And in that case we are ready. If he does not come, we have had a dress rehearsal in packing and will be more efficient stuffers for our real trip some day."

"You ladies are wonderful. You combine faith with reason, hope with reality, and the results are preparedness for a dream that just might come true. I like that. And since you have almost finished packing for our journey to freedom, I will pack a few clothes in my bag tonight, too."

Prayers of praise and thanksgiving ascended to the throne of God during our devotional time. Again everybody meditated on the beautiful words of Psalm 91:

Because he hath set his love upon me, therefore will I deliver
him: I will set him on high, because he hath known my name.
He shall call upon me, and I will answer him: I will be with
him in trouble; I will deliver him, and honor him.

"Give us wisdom to discern Your will, Lord." I heard these words, but it was rather difficult for me to concentrate that night. My mind was being abused by my thoughts. Gnawing questions continued to torment me. Where would we live if we left Lippehne? In some of the ruins Mutti told us about? It was only April and still cold outside at night. Here we at least had cozy beds. Would we have to sleep on the floor in some overcrowded building as the refugees in our school had to? Would we be overrun by tanks as many of them were?

When Mutti came to give me a good-night kiss, I tried not to let her sense my concerns. "I love you, too, Mutti," I responded to her good-night wishes, but pulling the warm feather coverlet over my head, I continued to think.

On Saturday afternoon Mutti's Polish friend brought the 10,000 zlotys and asked for the sewing machine. Mutti told her the machine was hers after we left and gave her a key to the house. "If we don't leave, I'll return your money to you."

Her friend was in agreement. She wished us a safe trip, gave Mutti a hug, and left.

Saturday night approached at a snail's pace, but finally the bundles and suitcases stood in the hall, packed for the next morning, and the clothes were neatly laid out—one little pile for everyone. Our food for the journey consisted of bread and two small milk cans, the bottom half filled with lard, and the top half with beet syrup. It was 9:00 P.M. now and pitch-dark outside. All the little ones were sleeping. No one had delivered papers.

"It looks as if we have been misled again," Mutti said sadly. "What does all of this mean?" She was really talking to herself, because nobody voiced an opinion. Were all of our hopes and dreams for the future dashed again? I detected sadness in the room. Nobody seemed to be breathing. Were they praying? What were they all waiting for so late at night? A miracle? How could anything happen now? I was beginning to feel sorry for all the adults. Was this really just a trap or a hoax? For two days we had been rushing around and for what? Just to sit and wait for nothing? Why didn't somebody say something? What are they thinking? This silence was torture to my mind. It felt as if everyone was waiting for death to knock on the door.

"Please say something!" I found myself bursting out.

"We don't know what to say," Mutti said very calmly, "we don't know what to say."

Suddenly—a knock on the front door. My heart crushed against my throat. I knew I couldn't speak now even if I wanted to.

"Was that a knock?" Onkel Emil asked.

"Yes, it was," Kaetchen answered.

Onkel Emil got up and hobbled to the door, the rest of us following behind. We stood in the hallway and listened, but there was no more knocking.

"We must have all been mistaken," Onkel Emil said, but decided to open the door anyway. I became scared when I saw a short, stocky person quickly glancing both ways on the dark street before entering.

"You have money?" he asked. "I have papers."

Mutti went to get the 10,000 zlotys, and handed them to Onkel Emil.

"I count money first." He counted out the bundle of money in the dim hallway light. "No, you not get papers. Papers cost 15,000 zlotys." Onkel Emil told him that the deal was 10,000 zlotys and we didn't have any more money. The stranger turned around to leave.

"Give 15,000 zlotys, then papers."

"We don't have more money. Good night," Onkel Emil said and walked the man to the door. Just before opening the door the stranger angrily yanked the money out of Onkel Emil's hand, shoved the papers at him, and slipped out of the house into the dark night. After the door closed, everyone stood in the hallway in total shock, staring at the papers in Onkel Emil's hand. He flipped through them exclaiming, "These are our tickets to freedom! This is the sign we have been waiting for! Rejoice!" Everyone was speechless. "Why aren't you happy?"

"I am just numb," Mutti answered, sighing deeply. "I can't believe it! Freedom is awaiting us! We will see our life's partners!"

Kaetchen stood in the hallway sobbing: "I can't believe it either, and I am so happy. But I am also sad. I must say good-bye to another place on earth that is so dear to me—the home of my parents."

After a short prayer meeting in the hallway, we carried the bundles and suitcases outside, placing them in the handwagon. Then Mutti and I double-checked on everyone's clothes for the next morning. I was going to wear two pairs of stockings, my boots, two dresses, a sweater, and a coat.

"Yes, I know you are going to be warm, Schaefle," Mutti said. "But we have to wear extra clothing just in case our bundles somehow get lost. You go to bed now. I'll wake you up at 3:30 A.M. so you can help me. Good night, Schaefle," and she kissed me.

I felt very strange that night. Sleep usually came quickly, but for a long time I lay wide awake. I thought of Kaetchen and her last night in her parents' house. She had spent her childhood here. Would she ever be able to return to Lippehne? Would I ever see these beautiful lakes again? Were we really going to leave tomorrow? I knew everyone was glad that the Lord controls our future, so I knew I should be, too. After all, it was only by the Lord's protection that we were still alive and well in Lippehne! No other Germans were. With that thought reassuring me, I drifted off to sleep at last.

19
Escape

It was Sunday morning, April 26, 1946. The darkness still hung about us, thick and heavy, as we left for the railroad station at 4:30 A.M. There was no way to muffle the noise of the handwagon as it rattled along the seamed sidewalk, but we encountered nothing out of the ordinary, arriving at our destination before 5:00. As we approached the station house, we noticed a group of nuns standing nearby with their arms raised while Polish men took their luggage and threw it on a pile of suitcases. I stood next to our luggage, wondering if the same might happen to us, when a controller came over to us to check our papers. He took our tickets and papers and vanished into one of the back rooms. Time stood still while we were awaiting his return.

"Why isn't he returning with our papers?" Kaetchen asked Mutti after we had waited quite a long time. The train was almost due to arrive. Suddenly he reappeared to tell us that specialists were not permitted to leave. He was yelling louder and louder to overpower the noise of the oncoming train.

"You can't leave. You are specialists."

"But we have permission to leave, don't you see that? And besides that, I have worked ahead so that the work will continue without me."

"Are you sure?"

"Yes, of course."

When the train came to a halt, he finally shoved the papers into Onkel Emil's hand and said, "Go!"

Mutti quickly lifted Udo and Marlies into the car and then helped Dieter. When she turned around, a man was running away with two of our suitcases. I saw him throw them on the luggage pile. Onkel Emil quickly retrieved them while the thief was busy stealing from other passengers, and flung them into the train. Mutti somehow managed to help Onkel Emil up the steps while the train was beginning to move. He stumbled and fell into the entrance of the compartment but quickly pulled himself up. "Thank you, Lord! Thank you, Lord! Thank you, Lord!" he rejoiced with the rest of our family.

Kaetchen and Mutti hugged each other, their faces wet with tears of joy as the train blew its whistle and pulled out of Lippehne.

All the children were excited about traveling by train.

"Mutti, I see the whole world going by real fast," Hanno bubbled. "All the trees are moving!"

"Why are the houses all fallen down?" Marlies questioned. None of the little ones waited for answers but, instead, fired question after question.

Happiness had taken hold of our group as never before. Everybody was joyous. Why then did I have to be plagued by fear? My heart was torn apart by fear. What would happen when the magistrate returned from his vacation today and discovered that we had left Lippehne? It would be no problem for him to come after us with an army jeep, catch up to us at one of the railroad stops, and take us back. What would our punishment be then? All of us, young and old, would probably have to go to that terrible jail Mutti was in. These thoughts took all the joy out of the trip for me. Wasn't it strange that none of the adults had mentioned this possibility? Was my fear unfounded? Why hadn't they thought about it? Yes, I knew the verses: "Trust in the Lord with all thine heart. . . . Be not afraid." I had heard these verses many times. That day, however, they offered no comfort to me at all.

"We are approaching Kuestrin," Mutti told us, "the town where I was captured and from which I escaped by running. What will befall us here today?"

"The Lord knows, Emmy. It won't be anything we can't bear," Kaetchen replied.

"I just wish we wouldn't have this long layover in Kuestrin. What are we going to do here until tomorrow morning?"

"If there is nothing for us to do, we'll have to wait and learn to be patient."

The train was slowing down, blowing its whistle and screeching to a halt. Fortunately our car stopped at the station building, and we didn't have to carry our belongings too far. After pulling, pushing, and dragging all of our baggage, we at last reached the waiting room. We walked in and found the room completely empty. There were no tables, benches, or chairs.

"We'll just have to settle on the floor," Onkel Emil said bluntly. "Why don't we all settle over there in that corner while Kaetchen and the boys stay in this corner. Let's all eat a little bread, and in the evening the children can stretch out on the bundles to sleep."

When dusk set in, men began to move about inside and outside the station building. One walked over to Kaetchen and offered to put all her luggage in safekeeping. He told her that Poles would come at night and steal things from her. He could help save her belongings by locking them into one of the station buildings and returning them the next morning before the train came.

"Don't do it, Kaetchen! No!" Onkel Emil intervened when he noticed that she seemed to be about to agree with the man. The man continued to talk to her and the children, and she finally gave him some of her things.

As the night lengthened, more creatures stalked in the darkness.

"Don't move—breathe quietly!" Onkel Emil whispered when the waiting room door opened again.

I had not yet slept a wink, and I didn't expect to because the door swung open constantly and shadows walked back and forth. We truly must have been under the Lord's wings because no one noticed us crouched in the dark corner. Nine of us were there, and we were all safe.

Suddenly we heard rifle bolts clicking outside, and when the door opened, my heart jumped. We were going to be shot. The magistrate had found us. I was right. These were Russians!

I could see the outlines of their fur hats! They knew we escaped and planned to cross the border—this would be the end for all of us. They were calling something into the room, but none of us moved. My whole body seemed to be paralyzed. The guns were clicking again, then there was silence for what seemed like an eternity. Suddenly they turned around and left.

The night seemed endless. We must have sat there on the floor for at least twelve hours, and it was still black outside. Oh, how we longed for morning! I couldn't stand the scuffling around of these creatures of the night.

A rough voice awakened me: "Frau, komm! Komm!"

Then Hanno screamed as if he was hurt.

"Frau, komm!" No, this was not a dream. A Russian wanted to rape Kaetchen. Hanno again screamed at the top of his lungs, and the soldier left abruptly.

"I told Hanno to scream," Kaetchen whispered. "My son saved me, with the Lord's help."

Finally light was beginning to encroach upon the darkness of the night.

"Thank you, Lord, for the morning light," I heard myself whispering.

We continued to cower in the waiting room until daylight flooded the filthy building.

"Our train is due soon," Onkel Emil said. "I suggest we all go outside and find the platform from which our train is leaving."

"Where is my friend from last night?" Kaetchen asked. "I think I told him when our train would leave, didn't I?"

And now we were all on the lookout for the Polish man but he was nowhere in sight. Several men came and offered their assistance again. One helped Kaetchen to the platform while she was carrying Vilmar. Another one wanted to help Mutti, but she refused his help. More and more men were encircling us, moving back and forth like vultures. I was in charge of one bundle and of Udo, who was carrying his pottie in his rucksack.

At last our freedom train slowly pulled into the station. Mutti again helped us children in first. As she prepared to lift a suitcase into the train, a man jerked it out of her hand and ran off with it. As another one said: "I'll help," he reached for two of our bundles and disappeared with them between the railroad cars.

Finally we had all boarded the train, and the steam engine pulled us out of Kuestrin.

"I have nothing left," Kaetchen said, "absolutely nothing. They took every single piece of my luggage. But praise the Lord! I have my two sons! 'The Lord giveth and the Lord taketh away, blessed be the name of the Lord.' " Holding her sons tightly, she began to weep.

The train moved slowly toward Berlin. At times it almost stopped.

"We must be changing tracks often," Onkel Emil reasoned. "We are making so little progress. Did you notice that we have passed some of the ruins twice?"

"Yes, I did," Mutti answered. "We seem to be zigzagging like a rabbit, except at the speed of a snail."

"What destruction! It was difficult for me to imagine such a horrible picture, Emmy," Onkel Emil continued. "Will Germany ever recover from all this devastation? How many thousands of people are buried under that rubble?"

"No one will ever know," Mutti concluded sadly. "And no one will ever know how many families have been torn apart by this war. No one knows how many children have been orphaned and how many parents have lost their children. I just marvel at the love God has shown to us."

"Yes, Emmy, you are truly blessed," and tears began to well up in his eyes.

"I am sorry, Emil. You will find your wife and daughters, too. We will continue to pray that you'll hear from your loved ones soon. You have done so much for Kaetchen and me in protecting us, and you have been such a friend and comfort to us. We just know that the Lord will reward you because He knows we can't. He will bring your family together."

"Mutti, look! Look up there! A bathtub is hanging there on the side of the wall. It is ready to fall. And I see half a bedroom with a dresser still standing there high up in that tall ruin. Where is the other half?"

"The other half, Dieter, is probably under the rubble. That must have been a beautiful home at one time. Look at the beautiful wallpaper and the pictures on the wall. I wonder where the residents of that home are today."

For miles we viewed nothing but the ruins of Berlin. This was the capital of Germany, one of it most beautiful cities. It had been founded in the year 1244. Gorgeous churches dating back to the year 1250, museums, opera houses, bridges, and monuments made it world-famous. The elevated and underground railway systems provided excellent transportation for its almost four and a half million people. Today we saw none of the old splendor. An occasional intact building here and there among the rubble was a rarity. Only a skeleton of the proud, German city was left.

"End station! Everyone please leave the train!" We heard over the loudspeaker after the train came to a halt. Kaetchen and her sons left the train first; then the rest of us followed.

"We are free! We are free! We are free!" Kaetchen called and passersby gave our group either a strange or a pitying look. "Where do we go now? We are free to go anywhere, but now we don't know where to go. That's funny, isn't it?"

"Yes," Mutti answered. "But we have prayed that the Lord would lead us to the right person, Kaetchen, and we believe that He will, right? But first, I think, we should thank the Lord for the air of freedom we are breathing right now. Do you realize it? We are free! Free! Free! Free of a system that daily caused us to live in fear and hunger. Free of a system that denied us all God-given, human rights."

"Thank you, Lord, for our freedom!" Onkel Emil prayed, while leaning on his cane with both hands. "Continue to lead us this day. We praise Your holy name. Amen."

We were still standing on the platform. There was no one else, only piles of rubble and debris. We didn't seem to be able to get our bearing. One thing, however, we *knew*: we were free!

Outside the station, we noticed a lady, wearing an armband with a red cross, walking toward us. She informed us that we could find temporary lodging at one of the refugee camps about four miles away. She gave us directions, and we started the long, tiring walk to the camp. After our arrival there, we were questioned thoroughly at the camp office about our home, relatives, plans for the future, and much more. All of the information was meticulously recorded. A young man then took us to the soup kitchen and offered us a bowl of soup and a slice of yellow bread.

"You are probably not familiar with this type of bread," he said, "are you? It is corn bread. The bread is baked right here by German people and the meals are also prepared here. The supplies are a gift from the Americans."

After our meal the young man showed us to our new home: a long wooden building with a flat roof.

"I am very sorry that we don't have nine beds close to each other. You will have to divide your group. Four of you can sleep in these two bunks right here, and the rest of you can make yourselves at home on those bunks along the wall over there. Here is one blanket for each of you. Have a good day! Auf Wiedersehen!"

Dieter immediately climbed on one of the top bunks and staked his claim. Because Udo and Marlies were small, they had to share a bottom bunk. As I was perched atop my new bed, I could see row upon row of bunks. Some people were sitting and staring at others, some were sleeping, and some were crying. Everybody seemed bored to death. Some men were snoring, and babies were crying. Younger children were singing, playing, and crying. How could anyone sleep here with all of this noise?

"Welcome to our community," an old man greeted us. "It is a one-room community. This room is home to four hundred of us. We have everything in common here. We have all lost our homes, we all sleep on burlap sacks stuffed with straw, we all eat the same watery soup. Many of us have lost loved ones on the treks and from the bombs. Many of us are sick. Dead are carried out of this building daily because of starvation, and we are all afraid of the person next to us. That person might take our clothes if we leave them on our bed at night. So, put your clothes under your straw at night," he rambled on. "And never leave any of your belongings alone. It is true what I tell you. Many of us have been here for a year. We have nothing to live for. We have turned into animals. Could you ever have imagined that Germans would stoop so low? The war has taken our homes, our families, and left us with nothing. And now the war has taught us to steal."

"No," Mutti said breathing deeply, "that is difficult for me to imagine. But do you know something? I have the feeling that the members of *this* family will survive this phase of their lives, too, because now we have freedom, and *that* is something we didn't have where we just came from. The freedom is worth more to us than the clothes on our backs and everything we had to leave behind."

Epilogue

Emmy Guddat's beliefs were to prove well-founded, though she and her four children would spend nearly another year and a half on their own. Kaetchen Mecklenburg was the first to have her family reunited. In May 1946, so weak from kidney and heart problems that she could scarcely walk, Kaetchen took her sons and hitch-hiked to Bochum, West Germany, the town mentioned in the mysterious letter. There, the first person she asked said, "Of course I know Wilhelm Mecklenburg!" He had established a great ministry in Bochum, confident that the Lord would return his family to him.

In later years the Mecklenburgs planted several churches in West Germany and one in Regensburg, Bavaria, before the Rev. Mecklenburg went to be with his Lord in 1982. Kaetchen still lives in Hameln, West Germany, carrying on an extensive counseling ministry. Hanno and Vilmar are married and both serve the Lord in their home churches.

As for Emil Schmidtke and the Guddats, Emil's daughter, Edith, was able to get them passes to West Germany through her work with the British occupational forces. After a relatively short stay of three months in Berlin, they all moved to Nienburg.

The conditions in the Nienburg refugee camp were much improved. The Guddat family was assigned to one and a half rooms that they shared with several other people. The camp kitchen, a half hour's walk away, served their soup every day. Dishes and water vessels were salvaged from the British army's garbage dump of tin cans, and Liane and Dieter were once again in charge of gathering firewood.

Onkel Emil's wife, Amalie, arrived unexpectedly in the Nienburg camp one day. Her health was broken from being forced to do heavy labor in communist stables. After enduring several cancer operations, she died in 1954. Her husband joined her in heaven in 1973. Emil's daughters still live in West Germany.

Emmy Guddat continued her attempts to contact Emil, her husband, but was repeatedly set back by such circumstances as not being able to obtain a single sheet of paper on which to write him a letter. After many months of frustration, the Guddats were reunited with their beloved Vati in the summer of 1947, in Nienburg, West Germany. However, eight more years of hardship and struggling still lay before them.

The Guddats remained in the camp less than two years before being moved to another nearby place in Nienburg that was not considered a "camp." But the new conditions were worse, even though Emil Guddat no longer had to sleep in a public hallway. The Guddats lived in a tiny, unheated room until 1952, under the tyranny of an abusive landlady. She didn't allow them to talk or sing out loud and did not want to give them permission to bathe in the house. Through the years of hand-to-mouth existence, the Guddats were sustained by packages of food and clothing sent by Emil's sister, who worked for the Liebenzell Mission in New Jersey. Much of what she sent had been donated by her American friends.

Little by little, the Guddats began to learn what had become of their various relatives. Seventy-eight-year-old Omi died of rape and abuse from the Russian soldiers shortly after the expulsion from Lipphene. She never reached freedom in the West. Liane's aunt made it to West Germany and eventually remarried. She died in May, 1987. The other set of grandparents died where they had lived, on their farm in East Prussia, not too long after the Russian occupation. Lithuanian Christians managed to get word of their death to the Guddats. Liane's ninety-three-year-old great-grandfather, they learned years later, had been found in a snow bank, shot by a Russian soldier.

Emil Guddat assisted a friend in founding the Baptist Church of Nienburg before he relocated and opened a store in Oberhausen. The business could not grow, however, due to the poor post-war conditions. Finally the decisions were made to come to the United States. Liane was the first of her family to enter New York Harbor, alone, on her 22nd birthday. "You will be our herald," her father had told her. Liane worked as a governess for a year, meeting her husband, Luther Brown, in Manhausset Baptist Church. Another friend from the same church sponsored the rest of the Guddats' ways to the United States in 1958, except for Dieter, who had immigrated to Canada the year before.

Emil Guddat worked for an import-export company on Long Island, and Emmy began work in an exclusive sweater shop in Locust Valley, eventually becoming the owner of the store. She used to say that she'd "always wanted just to walk under palms someday," and after their retirement, Emil and Emmy moved to Boca Raton, Florida, where they are still active in their church.

Today, Dieter has his own business in Toronto, while he and his family reside in Markham, Ontario. Marlies and her family live in Fort Lauderdale, Florida, and Udo, a high-school teacher, lives with his wife in Sea Cliff, New York. Liane, the author, and her husband lived in Owego, New York, until their retirement in July, 1987, after which they moved to Stuart, Florida.

Truly, the Lord does care for his own. The Guddats' story, while containing hardships and trials of which most people will never know anything, clearly shows the Lord's protecting hand on their family. While all around them other families were being killed or split up, dying of disease or starvation, and suffering untold horrors, the Guddats emerged into freedom, intact as a family unit and relatively healthy.

The full account of the miracles they experienced would fill several more volumes. In a 1987 letter to her publisher, Liane commented, "I had not envisioned how difficult it would be to sift through so many years of experiences and come up with just a few which might be a blessing to others." It is for the benefit of the "free world" that she has done so, however. Her abiding wish has been that no one would ever take the bountiful freedoms of the U.S.A. for granted.

"We still thank the Lord for bringing us to America," she says. "For it was only by His grace that we survived at all, and, even more, that we would be allowed to live among the most privileged people in the world."